The Boy from Hollow Hut

A Story of the Kentucky Mountains

Isla May Mullins

Alpha Editions

This edition published in 2021

ISBN : 9789355752178

Design and Setting By
Alpha Editions
www.alphaedis.com
Email - info@alphaedis.com

As per information held with us this book is in Public Domain.
This book is a reproduction of an important historical work. Alpha Editions
uses the best technology to reproduce historical work in the same manner
it was first published to preserve its original nature. Any marks or number
seen are left intentionally to preserve its true form.

Contents

A STRANGER AND A PROMISE	- 1 -
A PACKAGE BY MAIL	- 8 -
IN THE WILDERNESS	- 14 -
A HALT ON THE ROAD	- 18 -
A DOUBLE RESCUE	- 25 -
AN UNEXPECTED MEETING	- 33 -
A TRIP TO THE CITY	- 36 -
OPPORTUNITY	- 43 -
A STARTLING APPEARANCE	- 47 -
STEVE DEVELOPS A MIND OF HIS OWN	- 54 -
EXPERIENCE	- 63 -
LOVE'S AWAKENING	- 74 -
OLD TIES RENEWED	- 80 -
"ALL RIGHT, SON"	- 91 -
FLICKERING HOPE	- 97 -
IN THE CRUCIBLE	- 101 -
FRUITION	- 104 -

I

A STRANGER AND A PROMISE

The rabbit bounded away and was lost in the underbrush. Steve stood looking disgustedly after him, a limp figure, one shoulder dropping until the old knit suspender fell at his side, and a sullen, discouraged look settling in his brown eyes.

"I ain' no hunter noways. Peers lack I don't even know 'nough to ketch a rabbit," he said with scorn. "Whar's that lazy Tige anyways?" he added, his scorn merging into wrath.

Then jerking the old suspender in place he straightened up on his sturdy, bare feet, and darted through the underbrush in the direction where the rabbit had disappeared.

"I'll ketch you yit, yes I will, you same old cottontail," he muttered through clenched teeth.

There it was again! Just a moment the round, gray back darted above the bushes, and then plunging into deeper undergrowth, bounded on and on. But the slim, knotty brown legs plunged on and on too, till at last a swift, cruel stone felled the unlucky little woodlander, for Steve was a most skillful marksman.

"Huh! thought you'd git away from me, did ye?" said the boy, picking up the still body. "I reckons I kin do some things yit," he said, "ef I don't know much."

The boy was in a strange, new mood. He did not understand himself. Though a good hunter for a lad of twelve he had been heretofore a generous friend or conqueror of the fur and feathered folk, wont to deal gently with a fallen foe. Now he jerked up the limp body of the rabbit savagely and struck its head spitefully against a near-by tree trunk.

"I kin kill rabbits ef I can't do nothin' else."

Just then a big black and tan dog came into view with the dignity befitting age. Boy and dog had been born the same month, but while one was scarcely well entered upon life, the other's race was almost run. The boy was usually most considerate of the infirmities of his lifelong friend, but to-day he scolded the dog till with drooping tail and grieved, uncomprehending eyes he slunk away out of sight.

- 1 -

A strange experience had come to the mountain boy the day before which had changed his whole world. It was as though the wooded mountains which hemmed in his little cabin home had parted for a moment and given him a glimpse of a fascinating world beyond. He and Tige had wandered farther from home that day than ever before, though wanderers they had always been, the woods holding a deep interest for Steve. He loved to hide in the densest solitudes, lie still with his dog and dream, fantastic, unreal dreams. Now a definite, tangible vision had come to him out of the solitude of a hazy November day in the mountains of Kentucky. He had lain for two hours or more in the stillness when suddenly Tige lifted his head and gave a sharp bark, then came the sound of voices, strange voices Steve at once knew them to be, and as he caught the tones more clearly, recognized that one at least was of a kind which he had never heard before. Keeping Tige quiet with a firm hand, he lifted his head and listened with ear and soul, then into view stepped a man of medium height with a clean, fine face, clothes of a sort unknown to the boy, and an easy, alert stride totally foreign to the mountaineer's slouching gait. A mountain man accompanied him, but he too was a stranger to the boy.

The man of the new, strange species smiled at the boy's gaping mouth and wonder-wide eyes.

"Well, son," he said pleasantly, "are you a sportsman too?"

The quick, clear, cultured voice, the unfamiliar accent was so utterly foreign to anything the boy had ever heard that he could not take in the import of the words, and amazed silence was his only reply.

"Wal," drawled the mountain guide, "who'd er thought er seein' a chap lack that heah? Whar'd you come from anyways?"

This was familiar vernacular, and Steve, rising slowly from the ground, and allowing Tige to make friendly acquaintance with the strangers, said:

"I lives at Hollow Hut and I comes over here whenever I pleases. Whar'd you uns come from?"

The man gave a hearty but musical laugh at the ready dignity of the reply, but the boy's mouth dropped once more in consternation, as words came again in crisp, foreign accent.

"I came from the city, my lad, to get some of your fine quail and deer. You are willing I should have a few, are you not? My friend here is showing me the way."

The mountain folk had proved a most entertaining study for this sportsman, and his interest was ready for each new specimen encountered. Turning to the guide he said:

"Suppose we lunch here," and taking out his watch continued, "yes, it is high time; twelve thirty to the minute."

The boy stepped forward involuntarily for a look at the queer, pretty thing in the man's hand.

"What's that?" he asked.

"Why, that's a watch, son. Didn't you ever see one?" said the man kindly.

The guide smiled derisively: "Wal, I reckons not," while the boy, too interested for reply, asked again:

"What's a watch?" and the man with his genial laugh said:

"Son, we will be greatly pleased if you will take lunch with us. My name is Polk, Samuel Polk," he said, touching his cap with the unfailing courtesy of a true gentleman. "And after we eat I will show you the watch and tell you all about it."

But the mountaineer does not readily eat with "furriners," so Steve stood near by and looked on while the two men ate very strange things. Little cans were opened and tiny fish taken out that looked exceedingly queer. Mr. Polk, trying to persuade the boy to eat, explained that these were sardines, some square, white things were crackers, a thick stuff was cheese and that some big, round, yellow things were oranges. But Steve only stared in silence till the meal was over though Tige, with no instinctive handicap, accepted delicious scraps with astonishment and relish.

So amazed, however, had the boy been with it all that he nearly forgot about the watch. But when he remembered and the man let him take it in his rusty, brown fingers, that was the most wonderful moment of all. The tick, tick inside was a marvel, almost a thing uncanny to the boy, and when it was explained how the hands went round and round, telling the time of day, it surely seemed a thing beyond mortal ken.

The guide drawled out with a superior air: "Wal, sonny, you come from the backwoods shore ef you never heerd tell of a watch before."

The boy looked squarely at him in sullen resentment a moment, but with such opportunity at hand he wouldn't waste time with the likes of him. He asked, "What moves them things round?" and the man kindly opened the watch at the back and displayed all the cunning wheels which respond to the loosening spring, explained how it was wound each day to keep it from running down, and in answer to the boy's eager questions as to how such things were made told him something of watch manufacture.

At last the wonderful hour was over and the two strange men prepared to leave.

"Good-bye, son," said the man; "one of these days you will leave the mountains and go out into the big world to live a life of usefulness and honour, I hope."

The words, so simple and commonplace to the man, were to the boy like a telescope lifted to the unknown heavens, but through which he could not yet look. He watched the men go down the mountainside, the strange words which he did not comprehend, but was never to forget, ringing in his ears. A bit of heavy timber hid them at last, and the boy stood dejected a moment, his heart swelling with an agony of strange longing, while the dog looked up at him almost pleading to understand. Then suddenly, with a cry of hope, Steve sprang after them, the dog following. Breathless he came upon them, and the man turned in surprise at the tragic voice and face. When the boy could speak he panted out:

"I've got the bes' fox skin anywheres hereabout. I'll swap it with you uns fer that watch thing."

The man suppressed a smile and kindly replied:

"Why, lad, I couldn't do without it for the rest of this hunting trip, but I tell you what I will do. When I get back to the city I'll send you one."

"Then ef yer'll come home with me I'll give ye the fox skin now," the boy responded promptly.

"Oh, never mind about the fox skin now; I must get back to camp before dark and we are many miles away," said the man.

"But I can't take the watch 'thout you git the skin," said the boy sturdily.

"Well, now, I'll tell you," said the man, realizing that he had struck the stubborn, independent pride of a mountaineer. "You give me your name, tell me where you live and I'll send you the watch; then next time I'm over here I'll get the skin." The address was a difficult matter to determine, but the mountaineer helped them out.

This satisfied the boy and he saw the two strangers depart with better spirit, since he could look forward to the coming of the watch. He did not understand how it would ever reach him, but trusted the stranger implicitly. When the last sound of departing feet among the underbrush had died away, Steve turned and went home with long, rapid strides, the dog recognizing the relief and following with wagging tail.

He found supper on the table, the savoury bacon and hoe-cake greeting him from the door. The head of the family, lean, lank and brown, was already transporting huge mouthfuls from the tin platter to his mouth; the fat, slovenly daughter sat for a moment to rest and cool her face before beginning to eat, while the mother still occupied a chimney corner, pipe in mouth, for she "hadn't wanted nothin' to eat lately, her stomick seemed off the hooks somehow." These, with the boy, composed the family, a row of graves out under the trees at the back of the hut filling the long gap between Mirandy, a young woman of twenty-one, and Steve. The boy sat down, but before he ate that remarkable tale of his morning experience had to be told. When he was done the father said:

"Huh, better let city folks alone; don't have nothin' to do with none of 'em."

The boy, feeling the rebuke, then turned to his supper, but when his father had gone out to smoke, and Mirandy was in the lane looking for her sweetheart, Steve stole up to his mother's side and stood digging his toe in the sand hearth.

"Mammy," he said at last, "what makes that man diffrunt from we uns?"

The old woman smoked a moment in silence and then said:

"Wal, there's a heap over the mountains what makes him diffrunt,—things we ain' never seen ner heern tell on." She smoked again a puff or two, then added, "I recken schoolin's the most."

"What's schoolin'?" said the boy.

"Larnin' things," she replied.

The subject of schools had never been discussed in the boy's hearing. His father didn't believe in them, there wasn't a book, not even a Bible, in all the scattered little remote mountain community, and if the boy had ever heard either books or schools mentioned before the words had made no impression on him.

"Do they larn to make watch things thar?" he asked.

His mother said she supposed so, "she knew they larned out o' things they called books," and then she explained as best she could to him what schools and books were. When his father came in again Steve said boldly:

"Pappy, I'm er goin' over the mountains an' larn how to make them watch things."

The mountaineer stood as if paralyzed a moment, then his dull eyes blazed.

"No, you won't nuther! Not a step will ye go! Ye shan't nuver hev nothin' to do with no city folks, so help me God!"

The boy dropped back cowed and trembling; he had never seen his father so stirred. He didn't dare ask a question, but when the mountaineer had seated himself in the chimney corner opposite his wife, he continued:

"City folks with all their larnin', fine clothes an' fine ways ain't to be depended on. I wouldn't trus' one of 'em with a jay bird lessen I wanted to git shed of it. Don't you let me hear no mo' o' your goin' over the mountains arter city folks."

The prejudice of some mountaineers against the city is deep-seated. They have little use for the "settlements," meaning the smaller towns, but the city is their abomination. Jim Langly's prejudice was even stronger than that of the average mountain man of this type, for it had been a matter of contention between himself and his wife in the early days of their married life. She had always longed to see what was beyond the mountains and besieged him to go till the subject could no more be mentioned between them.

Steve soon climbed to his bed in a corner of the room with a very heavy heart. If city folks weren't to be depended on then he would never get that watch, and all the beautiful visions of learning to do things in a wonderful new world grew dim and uncertain. So heavy was his heart as he fell asleep that when he waked at daylight, it was with a terrible sense of loss and grief. The morning meal over he wandered off with Tige, dull and dejected, till the unlucky rabbit had crossed his path and stirred strange, resentful enmity towards his little familiar contestants of the woods. Sending the dog angrily off he skinned the rabbit with savage jerks and then carried it at once back to his home, saying:

"Fry it, 'Randy, fry it dog-goned hard."

His mother caught the sullen, angry tone, and when Mirandy went out in the kitchen to begin the dinner, she called him from where he sat on the door-step.

"Come here, sonny."

It was a rare term of endearment, and Steve got up quickly and went to her side.

"Don't think too much o' whut ye pappy said about city folks. He's allus hated 'em fer some reason, I don't know whut, 'less hit was 'cause I saw one when I was a gal afore we married, nuver min' how ner where, and arter that I allus wanted to see whut was over the mountings. Ef ever ye git a chanct I want ye ter go thar an' larn ter do things. I'd er done hit ef I'd er been a man. But don't say nothin' to ye pappy."

This caution was unnecessary; and what a change the simple words made for Steve! His spirit bounded up into the world of visions again, and when dinner was on the table he refused to take a mouthful of the savoury rabbit, so ashamed was he of the manner of its killing.

After this his mind was constantly on the watch which was to come. How it was to reach him he did not think out, for the simple reason that he knew nothing of the distance which stretched between him and the city, nor of methods of communication. No letter or piece of mail of any sort had ever come to his home, or that of any one else of which he knew but things of various sorts were gotten from the crossroads store ten miles away, skillets and pans, axes and hoes, which were made somewhere, and he supposed some time when some one of the community went to the store they'd find his watch there. But week after week went by till spring came on, and nobody went to the store. The mountain folk indeed had little need of stores. They spun and wove the cloth for their clothes, raised their corn, pigs, and tobacco, made their own "sweetin'," long and short, meaning sugar and molasses, and distilled their own whiskey. So the boy's heart grew heavy again with the long delay and he began to think bitterly that his father and not his mother was right, when one day a stranger whom he had never seen before drove up to the door.

II

A PACKAGE BY MAIL

"Howdye! Does airy feller named Stephen Langly live here?" said the stranger, reining in his tired, raw-boned steed without difficulty.

Mirandy went to the cabin door, stared a minute in surprise and then shook her head slowly. But Steve pushed past her saying:

"Yes, thar is, too. I'm Stephen Langly."

"You! Sakes erlive, I clean forgot that was yo' name!" and his sister laughed lazily, while the stranger joined in.

"Wal, you're a powerful little chap to be a-gittin' mail. But this here thing has yo' name on it, they tole me at the store, an' so I brung it along as I was a-comin' this-a-way. Hit's been thar mo' than three months they tole me."

Steve took the package, his hands trembling with eagerness and would have darted away to the woods with his treasure where he might look upon it first alone, but Mirandy stormed when he turned to go, and the man said:

"'Pears to me you mought show what ye got, when I brung it all this long ways to ye."

That did seem the fair thing to do, so when they had asked the man to "light and hitch," Steve sat down on the door-step and removed the wrappings from the square box; there was tissue paper first, a miracle of daintiness which the boy had never beheld before, and at last the watch came to view. Steve lifted it in trembling fingers, and while Mirandy and the man expressed their admiration his first quivering words were:

"That other one was yaller."

"Wal, now," said Mirandy, "that one was gold; you couldn't expect that man to send you no gold."

Mirandy, having a precious gilded trinket, was better posted on the colour and value of metals than Steve, though she made a slight error in her next statement.

"This hern is silver; that's the next thing to gold," and the bright nickel of the Waterbury twinkled in the spring sunshine as though trying to measure up to its admirers' estimate.

"A silver watch," said the stranger after he had heard the story of that autumn day with its promise of a watch which was just now fulfilled—"wal, you air a lucky boy, shore."

Mrs. Langly called feebly from within, and Steve went and laid it on the bed beside her. Her "stomick had never seemed to get on the hooks," as she expressed it, all winter; her spinning-wheel and loom had been long silent, and for a few days she had not left her bed.

Her eyes gleamed with strange, new fire as they fell upon the shining thing which belonged to another world from theirs, and when Steve had laboriously wound it, which he had not forgotten how to do, setting the wonderful machinery running, she whispered to him:

"Remember you air goin' whar you kin larn to make things lack that."

Steve's shining eyes answered hers, though the boy failed to catch the light of prophecy and final benediction which they held. Hugging his treasure, with no hint of oncoming change he went out to feed the stranger's horse while Mirandy prepared the dinner.

It was not until the visitor had gone and Steve was in the solitude of the woods with Tige that he found fullest joy in his new possession. It seemed to him he could never in all his life take his eyes from it again. He watched the hands go round and round, the little flying second hand, the more leisurely minute marker and the creeping hand which told the hours as they passed. Then again and again the back was opened and the busy little wheels held his breathless interest. He took no notice of Tige, but the old dog knew that his mate was happy and lay content beside him. Although for the first time in possession of a noter of the hours, he lost all account of time and did not move from the mossy bed where he had thrown himself until it was too late to see either hands or wheels. Then he called Tige to come and hurried back to his home to sit by the cabin firelight till Mirandy made him go to bed. The family all slept in the same room, three beds occupying corners; this main room and the lean-to kitchen constituting the whole house.

Steve's watch never left his hand the long night through, and for the first time in his uneventful life he slept fitfully, waking every little while to make sure it was there.

Jim Langly was away for a few days "to a logrolling" several miles away and did not return until dusk of the evening after Steve's watch came. The boy sat again by the firelight, watch in hand, when Jim walked in at the door. His eyes fell at once upon the strange, shining thing and his face was convulsed with sudden wrath:

"Didn't I tell ye to have nothin' to do with city folks? Ye shan't keep that thing. I'll smash it, so he'p me God!" But before he could lift a hand a scream came from the bed, and Mrs. Langly sat up wild and dishevelled.

"Let him hev it, Jim Langly, let him hev it," and then she dropped back gray and still. Jim Langly had seen that gray stillness before, and he stood looking upon it now in dumb terror. His wife had been ailing a long time, it was true, yet no one had thought of death. But the grim visitor was there in all his quiet majesty. The weary spirit, which had for so many years longed for flight into new haunts of men, had winged its way at last to a far, mysterious country of which she had heard little, but towards which for months past she had been reaching out with a strange prescience of which no one guessed.

It was a dreary night at the cabin. No one tried to sleep. Jim Langly said no more to Steve about the watch, and the boy wore it in his bosom attached to a stout string about his neck, keeping it out of sight, and sobbing in the stillness of the woods as he wandered with Tige, "Mammy wanted me to have it." And though his joy in it for the time was gone, there was peculiar comfort in this thought of her approval. The old dog looked up in the boy's face from time to time pitifully, or stuck his nose in the lad's hand, knowing well, in a way dogs have, what had happened.

Next day the wife and mother was laid to rest beside the row of little graves, and life completely changed for Steve. He went to bed as usual in his corner of the room, but he could not forget the still form which had lain in another corner the night before, and while Mirandy and his father slept heavily, he slipped from the bed, took a blanket and with Tige at his heels went into the woods again. Here in the stillness which he loved, worn out with loss of sleep and his first encounter with grief, nestling close to old Tige slumber came and held him until late the next day. His father and Mirandy paid little attention to what he did, so night after night he took his blanket and dog and slept in the woods, the two only going to the cabin for meals.

During all these strange, restless days the words of Steve's mother came to him over and over: "Remember you air goin' whar you kin larn to make things lack that watch." And he thought, "How am I a-goin' lessen I jes' go?" He knew his father would never give him permission, it was not worth while to ask it, so gradually his plans took shape in the solitude of the woods with no one to counsel. Had the boy known what distance lay between him and his goal he would have grown faint-hearted, but he had no conception of what his undertaking meant. So he laid his plans with good courage, which plans, of course, included the taking of his dog. For three or four days Steve took an extra share of corn pone and bacon, Mirandy not noticing in her shiftless manner of providing, and feeling the loss of her mother, she was even more listless than usual. These extra rations for himself and Tige Steve carried to the woods and laid away. Then his beloved fox skin, the greatest treasure which he possessed beside the watch, he must take that with him, because it was "the man's"; he had promised it in return for the watch, and now that he was going he must take it along to give to the man. The boy had no thought of any difficulty in such a search. The food, the skin, the watch, and the scanty clothes he wore constituted all his equipment for the journey. When he started out with the skin Mirandy lazily asked what he was going to do with it, and he replied: "Use it fer a piller in the woods."

"Ye better quit sleepin' out thar," she said; "somethin' 'll eat ye up some night."

"I ain't a-feerd," he said, and she thought no more about it.

Three days passed with a good accumulation of food, and as Steve and Tige lay down to sleep at night the boy said:

"Tige, we've gotter be a-goin' 'bout day arter ter-morrer," and the dog wagged sleepy assent. But next morning when Steve wakened a peculiar stillness smote him. Tige was usually alert at his least move. With intuitive alarm Steve put out his hand,—and touched a rigid body! Drawing back he sprang to his feet, a cry of anguished appeal on his lips:

"O Tige, Tige, ye ain't dead too?"

But death makes no reply. His lifelong playmate lay straightened out in that last unalterable, mysterious sleep.

The boy was too stunned for tears. He knelt beside his dog in silent misery. After a long while he rose from the ground and going to a moss-covered rock near by where laurel and forget-me-nots blossomed and rhododendron bells hung in clusters, with a stout stick and his sturdy hands he dug beneath the rock an opening large enough to hold his dead dog. Then he went back to where his old playmate lay, and lifting the stiffened body in his arms he stumbled blindly to the rock and laid it away.

Towards evening he slowly made his lonely way home.

Mirandy, missing the dog at last, inquired: "Whar's Tige?" and Steve's stiff lips articulated the one word, "Dead."

She replied indifferently, "Wal, he want no 'count any mo'. I reckons hit's a good thing."

Steve had no answer and with swelling heart made his way to the woods to sleep alone. It was long before he could sleep, and as he lay in the unbearable loneliness, he decided that next morning he would start on that journey to the unknown. Perhaps to that new world sorrow would not follow! He would not need so much food now; he had enough saved already. The death of the dog urged him on to his purpose as nothing else could have done.

He went down to the cabin next morning for the last time. It was a warm spring morning. Passing Mirandy sitting on the door-step, her breakfast dishes not yet washed, he paused a minute, longing to say something, for although the bond between them was of blood and not of the heart, yet she was part of the life from which he was tearing himself away, and he longed to sob out a good-bye. But he must not, so choking down words and tears he stumbled off, never once looking back. His father sat in the chimney corner smoking his morning pipe, but father and son had always lacked interests in common, and the coming of the watch had put an insurmountable barrier between them. So Steve's only thought in passing him had been to escape suspicion. It was to his mother that the boy had always shyly told his day-dreams in the woods,—dreams which reached out into a wonder world lying beyond the mountains. And she had smoked her pipe in silent sympathy, occasionally asking: "Did ye see big houses, rows and rows of 'em on land, and some a-ridin' the water? I've hearn tell of 'em in my day," so furnishing inspiration for more dreams in the future.

"O Mammy, O Tige," sobbed the boy when safe at last in the woods, and he threw himself down in an agony of weeping beside the rock where the old dog lay buried. When calm at last, he took up his bundle of bread and bacon wrapped about with his fox skin, and started slowly away. He took no thought as to direction, he was simply "goin'," as his mother had told him. A dismal rain soon set in, but on and on he persistently tramped all the long day, water dripping from his ragged trousers and old hat as he went farther and farther away from all he had ever known. He met no one, saw no habitation anywhere, only the startled denizens of the wood scurrying here and there out of his path. Over mountains and across ravines he went on and on. He was puzzled and discouraged when night dropped down, and his aching feet and tired legs said he must have travelled many miles. "Shorely I'll git thar to-morrer," he said, as he lay down upon his fox skin, but another weary day of tramping over unknown ways without sight of any human being brought terror to his sturdy heart and when he lay down alone at night he felt that he was the only human being in the universe. Oh, if he only had Tige!

All the people he had known and those he expected to see beyond the mountains seemed to have sunk into some great unseen abyss. He could never find his way back to the old cabin, he knew, and he began to feel that he could never reach forward to the wonderful city of which he had dreamed. In the agony of loneliness and the chill of night which settled upon him he cried again, "O Tige, O Mammy!" Did the tender mother-arms reach down and draw her boy near to the heart of God? At any rate he grew quiet. He remembered vaguely that he had heard how God is everywhere, and with a new strange sense of companionship with the great Creator, which comes to souls in extremity, he fell asleep and did not waken until the sun, bursting forth with new brilliance after the day of rain, had lit up the mountain tops and set the birds to singing.

He enjoyed the breakfast of very hard corn pone and bacon, and took out his beloved watch. The busy, little shining thing, which he never forgot to wind, did not mean much to him as a marker of time, for he knew little about the hours as enumerated by the watch, but it was on this morning of new courage a fresh pledge of wonderful things awaiting him. He started on again with steady strides, and tramped bravely till mid afternoon without adventure.

Suddenly, without premonition, his heart thrilled at faint sounds which seemed marvellously like those of a human voice. He stood still a moment in an agony of uncertainty, straining eye and ear for confirmation.

Yes, he was right! He caught the crackle of dry twigs and underbrush, while the faint human tones grew clear and distinct. Under the discipline of loneliness and distress the face of the untutored boy beamed with eager welcome which held no reserve and caught no suspicious glimmer of lurking treachery as near-by bushes parted and steps were close upon him.

III

IN THE WILDERNESS

Two men were before him, men very similar in appearance to those Steve had known, though with something in their faces which made him draw back even in the moment of joy at meeting others of his kind.

"Sakes erlive, Bub, whar'd ye come from?" called the taller, harder looking of the two.

"I come from Hollow Hut," answered the boy with his simple dignity.

"And whar you goin' to?" called the other man, while both laughed unpleasantly.

"Ter the city," said the boy.

"Wal, now, that's a pretty nice fox skin ye got rolled up thar," said the tall one as they came closer. "S'pose you jes' hand that over to us."

"I can't," said the boy, holding it tighter in real alarm. "I swapped it with a man fer a watch, an' I'm a-takin' it ter him."

"Is that so!" exclaimed the tall man. "So you've got a watch, hev ye? Who'd a-thought it,"—and they both haw-hawed loudly. "Now, ye can jes' han' that over too, fer we mean bizness, don't we, Bill?"

And with that they pounced upon the terrified boy, jerked the fox skin from his clinging fingers and soon brought forth from its hiding-place in his bosom the beautiful, beautiful watch! Steve fought like a small tiger, but he was no match for them and stunned and bruised he soon lay upon the ground while the two men walked off, never once looking back at their helpless victim.

For a few minutes Steve could not think, so severe had been their cruel blows; then indignation, such as he had never known in his life, swept over him in a sudden flood. He sprang to his feet, ignoring pain and keenly watching which way they went, stealthily followed after. For two hours he kept within hearing of them, though being careful always that they did not get a glimpse of him. He did not know what he was going to do, but when they finally halted for the night he halted too. The men had also taken the last of his corn pone and bacon; there was nothing for him to eat, but he did not even think of it, so intently was he listening. Soon they began to sing and laugh very loudly and he knew then they had plenty of whiskey with them. Hope rose in his heart. After a bit they would fall into heavy sleep. He knew well the ways of drink.

Soon all was still, and after waiting a while till the sleep was deep he crept upon them. Fortunately the moon was up in its full glory and Steve could see plainly what he was about. He crept up close to the two snoring men and across the feet of the tall one lay his fox skin.

"I must git that anyways," said the boy to himself, "for it belongs to the man in the city."

Slowly, cautiously he lifted it from the big heavy feet, and there was not a stir. Then he stood, his heart almost bursting with longing for his watch. It was in the big man's pocket he was sure, and he stooped close a minute, reaching out a hand,—but he didn't dare. If he waked them, skin and watch would both be gone, and he must by all means get the skin to give to the man in the city. He went sorrowfully away with only the skin. He didn't dare stop near them, so he tramped half the night in spite of frequent twinges in his left ankle which had had a little twist as the men threw him down, and at last the boy dropped upon the ground, utterly exhausted, to sleep until noon next day.

When he wakened, stiff and sore from the blows of the men, and tried to get upon his feet he found that left ankle so swollen and painful he could not put the foot to the ground. He realized for the first time also with great consternation that he had nothing to eat. Bruised, sore, empty, helpless he sat alone in the woods. But even then he did not know the desolation of the night before. He felt once more that comforting sense of companionship with the great Creator, and he faced the situation sturdily.

He crept about on his knees hunting berries which he knew were good to eat. It was a laborious way to get breakfast, or more properly dinner, but he succeeded in finding enough to still somewhat the gnawing in his empty stomach, and suddenly as he lifted his head a road lay before him. With hope that was almost a tranquil certainty he crept to the roadside and sat down. An hour or more passed with only the call and song of birds to break the stillness,—when, list! There was surely a rumble of wheels! And then the cry came distinctly, "Git up thar!"

Tears of joy rained down the boy's face as a covered wagon drawn by four mules came into view, though he sturdily brushed them aside as the wagon drove up and halted.

"Hello, thar," called a lusty youthful voice, and the driver, a young fellow of perhaps nineteen who was mounted on one of the mules, turned round and saw at a glance the swollen, helpless foot.

"Done up, air ye, Bub? Whar do ye belong anyways?"

Steve knew at once that these people were friends, and told them his little story.

"I want to git to the city, so's to give the skin to the man thar an' then I'm goin' to larn to make watches an' things," he concluded.

"Wal, you air a long piece from the city, but we uns kin help ye git to the railroad and that'll take ye to the city."

Several heads of varying sizes were sticking out of the wagon by this time, and when Steve had been helped in among the occupants he found it was a family moving from one little hamlet to another. The husband and father had recently died and they were going back to their mother's home to live among her "kin."

The kindly mother at once bound up Steve's injured foot with white of egg and salt, which she said would "fetch it round all right," and hearing the empty rumbles of his poor little stomach she said she didn't believe "thar was a thing inside of it," and proceeded to give him a good square meal.

Was there ever anything happier than to be driving along the road with a comfortable foot, a full stomach and in the midst of friends! Steve had never known greater joy than that moment held. They were a "happy-go-lucky" family he had fallen in with,—and for the first time in his life he was in the midst of the merry banter of children. The mountain folk of remote regions lack a sense of humour, and Steve had grown up entirely alone, the cabins of Hollow Hut being scattered, so he sat through the afternoon in a maze of delight. There were snickers and giggles, punching in the ribs and tickling of toes from these children who lived on the border of civilization, for Steve had really gone blindly towards his goal.

As they drove gaily along Steve heard a sudden rumbling which suggested thunder, the children cried, "The train, the train," and stopping the mules quickly the big brother who was driving jumped down, while three of the children sprang out with a bound and all grasped the bridles at their heads. It was done so quickly there wasn't time to ask a question and then a monster came tearing, puffing, hissing past them. Steve's eyes almost started from their sockets and when it was past he sank back limp and quivering.

"Why, chile, didn't ye nuver see no railroad trains afore?" said the good mother.

Steve managed to say, "No," and then the children told him all the astonishing things about railroads. To his mingled joy and terror another came along from the opposite direction when they had driven on about a mile further, and this time it came more slowly, making a full stop near them.

"Whut air they a-doin' that for?" asked Steve, and when it was explained that they had stopped for fuel or water, there being no station near, a quivering light broke over his face, and remembering his watch as his mind tried to grasp new sources of motion, he said:

"They're jes' a-stoppin' to wind hit up, then."

Very soon after this they came to a cabin by the roadside and all the family within poured out to see the strangers.

"Won't you light and hitch?" drawled the man of the house, but the boy driver refused, saying they wanted "to git to their kin afore night." He suggested to Steve, however, that if he wanted to go to the city he had better stop there, for they were going further from any station than he would be there. The folks of the cabin were hearty in their invitation to the boy when they had heard his story, even the fact of his probable helplessness for a while not marring the beauty of their royal hospitality. So Steve was carefully lifted out and helped in among new friends.

The little cabin was full to overflowing with boys and girls, one girl of fifteen fondling her baby as she would a big doll, in ignorant, unlawful, and one perhaps should say innocent motherhood. She, a waif herself, had come along needing shelter and they had taken her in.

When Steve had had his supper pallets were spread everywhere about the cabin floor upon which the family went to rest fully clothed, after the fashion of mountaineers, and to the boy the night was a great contrast from the previous one in the loneliness of the woods. He thought of his own home as he had never done since he left it, wondering if his father and Mirandy would like to see him, but he never dreamed of how they had searched the woods for miles around when he was missed the second day after leaving. His failure to return the first day and night they thought little of, for he frequently did not come back after morning, but the second day's absence had brought real alarm, and when they found his blanket Mirandy said she knew something had killed and eat him up; she had forgotten about the fox skin which in that case should also have been there. But Jim Langly set his teeth grimly and said the boy had gone off "along o' that watch," and he did not cease to make inquiry as he had opportunity, trying to trace his son, while he angrily threatened to kill that city man if ever he "showed up agin in them parts."

IV

A HALT ON THE ROAD

Steve spent a week in the crowded but hospitable cabin of his latest friends resting the swollen foot. It was not seriously sprained and would have given him no trouble but for the long tramp upon it the night before and his general fatigue.

He had an interesting time with this family on the roadside. They were of the most shiftless type of mountain folk. Life was a long holiday to them, every meal a picnic. There were too many to gather about the table in the little log lean-to, so the elders only sat down at meal times. The children came up shuffling, pushing and squirming good naturedly to get their portions and ran away again full-handed to sit on the door-step or flat upon the ground outside while they ate. Sometimes one ambitious consumer would succeed in disposing of his viands more rapidly than the others and then woe to some small delinquent! His food would be snatched away and a lively fisticuff probably follow during which the inevitable "yaller dog" was usually the gainer. The disturbance at times reached a height which brought the mother lazily to the door with a mild:

"Now ef ye alls don't quit fussin', I'll set the boogers arter ye ter-night," which was a dire and telling threat, for, to the mountain children, "boogers" meant ghosts, witches, hobgoblins, thieves, or any other terrible, mysterious creature of the night.

Steve went up to the table with the rest for his portion of food, and took his chances with the other children if a squabble began. Association with the children was most enjoyable to Steve. They told marvellous tales about giants and mountain feuds and the mother's threat of "boogers" was sure to stir up all their recollections about ghosts. Wherever there was a "killin'" as the result of a mountain feud ghosts were sure to congregate and marvellous were the tales which clustered about each bloody spot. Steve being a new listener must hear all these old tragic stories.

When meals were over, the family disposed themselves to their liking. The head of the house invariably lit his pipe and sat in the chimney corner to smoke, a custom quite familiar to Steve. The mother washed the skillet and few utensils used about the meal, smoking her pipe the while. The young girl sat down outside in the sun to play with her baby, the big boys perhaps went off hunting and the children wandered aimlessly in and out.

The fields of corn and tobacco had been planted and now there was little to do but watch it grow, so they thought. The hogs practically took care of themselves. What more could any one demand, a blank look would unconsciously have inquired, if asked why they did not work.

When the day was over and the troop of children began to grow sleepy, one after another dropped down upon the cabin floor, perhaps upon a pallet, perhaps not, and fell asleep. The older ones followed in the same way, as inclination suggested, and room was cheerfully made for Steve among the rest. For a night or two the full chorus of audible breathing wakened him frequently, but he soon became accustomed to it.

In the morning the voice of some child was apt to be heard first:

"Mammy, I'm hongry."

And the reply would come, "Now you shet up, 'tain't time ter be gittin' up yit," or perhaps the satisfied parent would yawn and say:

"Wal, I reckons I might as well git up and stop ye mouth," and so the household would gradually emerge from slumber.

This was the normal daily life, but comedy and tragedy came to them as to the rest of the world, and Steve had a taste of both during his stay of a week.

Unlike Hollow Hut it was a somewhat thickly settled community and one moonlight night some young folks from neighbouring cabins came in. Steve's friends made the visitors welcome and hailed with delight the banjo which one of them had brought. The young folks were out for a frolic and laugh and joke were ready.

Pretty soon the banjo began to tune up and set everybody's feet to patting.

"Clear out things," called one of the boys, and in no time the few articles the room held were out of the way. Then the air vibrated with "Hook and Line," "Sourwood Mountain," and other lively tunes, while everybody danced except Steve, who crept to the farthest corner and in wonder looked and listened. He had never seen dancing or heard music before.

The girl with the baby came and dropped it down upon his lap while she joined in the fun, and it almost seemed that the cabin itself would break from its moorings in the abandon of rollicking, swaying motion.

When everybody was tired out the banjo player, a young fellow with deep-set black eyes and the unmistakable look of an artist in embryo, swung into a monologue accompanied by the banjo, part talk, part song, describing a fox hunt which was most fascinating and altogether remarkable.

He called the hounds with "Here Tige," "Here Jack," "Here Spot," "Here Bob-tail," interspersed with the tooting of a horn, long musical whistles and the banjo striking soft staccato chords. He mustered the men, he raced the horses with excited calls of "Git up thar," and gave clever imitation of fleeing hoofs, "to-bucket, to-bucket, to-bucket," in a rapid, low, chanting song. Then the leading hound opened with a plaintive bay "how!-oo-oo-oo, how!-oo-oo-oo," and one by one the others joined in with varying notes till it swelled to a weird chorus of baying hounds which the banjo and the musician's voice made most realistic. Next the fox was spied and there were cries of "Hello! Ho! Here he is!" "There he runs," with the banjo thumping like mad! Then the medley shaded down into a wild, monotonous drumming from the strings and the voice, which represented most thrillingly the chase at full height. At last the fox was caught with dogs barking, men calling, and banjo shrilling a triumphant strain in stirring climax.

Steve followed it all in breathless excitement, and the rest of the audience received it with boisterous enthusiasm.

After this somebody started the lovely old ballad, "Barbary Allen," in which all joined; then, "I have a True Love in the Army," and "The Swapping Song" followed, while "Whistle up your Dogs, Boys, and Shoulder your Guns," made lively the leave-taking and echoed back from far down the road.

Then there was a night of tragedy during Steve's visit. The sleepers of the cabin were suddenly aroused by blood-curdling whoops and yells, gunshots, racing horses and running men. Everybody was instantly alert and the family turned out of the cabin en masse. It was thrilling. All knew well what it meant. The head of the house and older boys joined the fleeing crowd like dogs in a chase.

"That's Bud Levit's folks and the Cuneys done broke out agin 'bout that ole fuss, I bet," drawled the wife and mother, when the tumult had died down to faint echoes.

"I reckon thar'll be a big killin' this time," said one of the children with zest.

"Thar shore was a passle er folks and a pile er shootin'," said another enthusiastically.

"Now, you-alls git back to bed an' shet up," said the mother, and her brood gradually quieted down.

Next day when the man of the house and older boys returned about dark, full of whiskey and full of talk, a most exciting tale was unfolded to the eager listeners.

"Hit was the biggest killin' whut's been in these parts fur many er day," said the man with pride. "I'll tell ye when they did git together they fit lack beastes.

When ev'ythin' was over thar was five on 'em a-layin' in their blood. Three of the Levits an' two of the Cuneys."

"Wal, I hope they'll keep quiet fer a spell now," commented the woman.

Then all the ghastly details were gone over with the children listening eagerly, drinking it in as they would a story of an exciting hunt. When the children discussed it afterwards one little fellow said to another: "I tell yer what, I'm er goin' ter be a fighter jes' lack them Levits. I'll shoot 'em down ef anybody comes foolin' round me."

Steve listened soberly. The experience was not a new one to him, but he remembered that his "Mammy" had always said she didn't like killings and that mountain folks ought to "larn better some way." The words came back to the boy with peculiar meaning since the voice which uttered them was still. He said nothing, but it all made him more anxious to move on towards that other world of which he and "Mammy" had dreamed.

The following morning his foot seeming fully restored and clearing weather having come after several days of rain, Steve said "he thought he'd move on."

"Whar ye goin'?" said the man of the house who had paid little attention to him before.

"I'm er goin' to the railroad fust, an' then from thar to the city to give the fox skin to the man, an' to larn things."

"Larn things," said the man scornfully, not being in the best of humour after the previous day's dissipation. "Huh! I s'pose ye'll be goin' to some er them city schools. Ye better go on back whar you come from. Schoolin' ain't no good ter anybody. Hit's them schools whut larns folks to go 'round pesterin' other folks, breakin' up 'stills.' Folks has got jest as good er right ter make whiskey es anything else," which showed in what he was especially interested.

Steve made no answer for the man was too forbidding in his irritability, but the boy kept to his determination to press on at once towards the railroad. After breakfast was over he went back to see the woman of the house, and in lazy kindness she said she wished she had a little bread and meat to give him but "there wan't none left," which Steve was quite prepared to hear, for there were many mouths to feed and never any left.

"I hope ye'll git thar all right. I reckons ye'll git somethin' to eat on the road, and ef ye're ever to come this-a-way agin come an' see us," she drawled as she smoked.

"Ye been mighty good ter me," said Steve, "an' I ain't nuver goin' ter forgit it."

He passed the children about the door-step, his fox skin under his arm, and they stood and watched him leave with a sort of sorrowful solemnity. Goodbyes are a thing unknown to mountain folk.

Then he walked off without much thought as to direction, having a definite impression, however, as to the way he should go, which was part instinct and partly remembrance of what the boy on the moving wagon had told him. The people he had left were too inert to think of giving him any instructions. But down the road he passed the big boys of the house sitting idly by the roadside. They had heard with satisfaction their father's opinion as to Steve's going in search of "larnin'." As Steve came in sight one of them nudged the other and said, "Less throw him off the scent."

"Which-a-way ye goin', Bub?" he asked when Steve came up.

Then for the first time Steve stopped and thought.

"Why, that-a-way," he replied pointing.

The big boys laughed boisterously. "Ye'll nuver git to no railroad goin' that-a-way. Thar's the way ye want ter go," said one, pointing off at a slightly different angle, which made the greatest difference in the boy's ultimate destination.

Steve looked doubtfully, but when he reflected a moment he remembered that he really did not know positively in what direction to go.

"Is that so?" he inquired looking earnestly at the boys.

"Hit shore is," returned both of them.

"How fur is it?" asked Steve.

"Oh, 'tain't fur," said one of the boys; "ye ought ter git thar before night easy. You go straight as a crow flies that-a-way," pointing as he had before, "and ye'll come to the railroad tracks. Ye can't miss hit fer ye're bound to cross 'em, an' ef ye go straight, lack I tell ye, ye'll be right at the station."

The boy on the moving wagon had described the railroad tracks to him, so Steve started off feeling reassured, and it never occurred to him that any one could be mean enough to misdirect him. It was a pity the echoes from the boisterous laughter of the boys when he was out of hearing could not have reached the little traveller's ears, but they did not, and Steve pressed on with good spirits feeling that he was almost in sight of his goal with less than a day's journey before him.

He turned at once from the road and went on and on, knowing as well as the crow how to keep straight with the compass, although like the crow he had never heard of one. The straight path took him quickly into the wilderness, but that did not dismay him as wilderness travel had become most familiar to him. At noon he began to feel so empty, he longed for just a little piece of corn bread. And then remembering that the mother thought he'd get something to eat on the road he began looking cheerfully for the smoke of a cabin somewhere. He had been vaguely disappointed at striking no road anywhere, but he had not asked the boys any particulars as to the route. Everything so far in his journeying had been unexpected, and the possibilities of routes were so totally unknown to him that he had started on again, as when he left home, unquestioning.

The empty stomach continued to cry loudly for food as the afternoon wore on, and no cabin smoke gave token of life anywhere. He did not suffer from thirst for mountain streams and springs were abundant. He pressed bravely forward, cheering himself with the thought that the boys had said he would come to the tracks before dark. But twilight began creeping in among the forest trees and still no tracks were in sight. Anxiously he listened for the terrible yet thrilling rush of a train which he remembered so well. He ought to be in hearing distance of them by now. But nothing broke the forest stillness save the twitter and song of birds, the scurrying of rabbits or frisking of squirrels with occasionally the sound of some larger animal in the underbrush.

Finally night fell with the poor boy straining his anxious eyes for the shining tracks of which he had heard. He forced his aching limbs along till suddenly, with a quivering sob, his strength seemed all to go and he sank upon the ground in a pitiful heap. He was too exhausted to think and in a few moments was sound asleep.

He lay upon the summit of a rugged mountain, which dropped precipitately down just beyond the sleeping boy, to ripple off again in lesser lofty heights, with beautiful fertile valleys and tossing streams between. A little, lonely, helpless human soul he lay upon Nature's majestic bosom, with the Infinite hand beneath his head.

In the morning when he waked billows of mist in silver splendour were rolling slowly from the valleys below, like Nature's incense rising in her sacred morning hour.

Although born in the mountains the mystic grandeur of the scene filled Steve with awe. Rising, he gazed, a part of the worshipful silence, and then as the sun burst suddenly into golden glory above the waves of mist, his mind as suddenly seemed to shoot up from the mists of fatigue and sleep. It was the peculiarly clear brain which sometimes comes with long abstinence from food. Instantly he knew that he had been fooled!

- 23 -

Turning to look back over the way he had come he said to himself: "Them boys told me wrong, an' they did hit a purpose. They're lack their pappy, they don't want to larn nothin' an' they don't want nobody else ter nuther."

V

A DOUBLE RESCUE

The boy stood quietly on the mountain top and took his bearings. He knew the way he had come, and remembering his previous impressions, and what his friend on the moving wagon had said, he turned at last and started down at an acute angle from the direction he had come. He gathered again as he went whatever he knew to be good to eat in the way of berries and herbs, but he soon began to feel so weary that he could hardly drag himself along. Had he gotten out of the wilderness only to plunge into it again and be lost? For as the day went on and he met no one, saw no cabin or the long-looked-for railroad tracks, discouragement and anxiety beset him. Noon passed again. Sometimes he thought he must stop and rest, but he was afraid if he did he could never get up again. His fatigue and hunger were far greater than in his previous experience in the wilderness, for he had never eaten heartily at the roadside cabin, knowing that food was not abundant there. So he was not in the best of trim for a long fast and great physical strain.

The remnants of his courage were wearing away when at last he seemed to be emerging into a more open country. He was still in the woods, but there was a subtle difference. He felt somehow that man was in proximity somewhere, though he had as yet seen no sign. His pulses quickened a little, and then suddenly a child's scream rang out.

Steve bounded forward at first with joy, and then as scream after scream followed, with the unmistakable agony of fear in the cry, forgetting his deadly weariness he ran swiftly in the direction of the sound, dropping the fox skin as he ran. In a breathless moment he came in sight of a good sized tree, and hanging from a high limb by the skirt of her dress was a little girl, head downward.

Steve saw in an instant that she could not help herself, and that she might fall to her death any moment. He did not pause or hesitate. Up the tree he went, his bare feet clinging to the sides, up and up in a twinkling, then he carefully crept out upon the limb and drew the little girl safely up beside him.

"Oh," she said when she had recovered her equilibrium and gotten her breath, "I thank you so much," and even then Steve was conscious that he had never seen anything so pretty in all his life as the blue eyes which looked up into his, and the soft yellow curls which framed her little face. But he hurried to get her down safely. With infinite care he helped her until she could go on down the tree alone, and then, he did not know what happened, but things suddenly seemed to whirl round and he fell to the ground in an unconscious heap.

The next he knew some one was wiping his face with a damp cloth and chafing his hands. He was too tired to open his eyes and see who it was. Then a woman's voice was saying in a worried but gentle tone:

"What were you doing in the tree, Nancy? You know I don't like for you to climb trees."

"Why, mother," replied a frightened little voice, "I found a poor little birdie out of its nest, and I pinned it up tight in my apron pocket and carried it up the tree and put it into the nest. The father and mother bird were so worried about it. I didn't know I was going to fall, and make this boy fall too, and hurt himself so bad," and the small voice broke pitifully.

"You never should have tried to do such a thing," said her mother firmly, and then as the little voice went into sobs, Steve opened his eyes in a brave effort to try to assure them he was all right.

"Oh, I'm so glad you are better," exclaimed the woman who knelt beside him.

She looked so kind and nice that Steve struggled to get up and further reassure her, but there seemed weights holding him down and a sharp pain thrust through and through his left arm.

"I am afraid you have broken your arm," said the woman anxiously. "Nancy, you run right over to the store and get your father," she said to the little girl. And Steve watched a white pinafore and flying yellow curls through a half-conscious dream mist, with a satisfied sense that he was at last in the new world of his visions.

And he was, for he had stumbled blindly through a bit of wood at the back of Mr. Follet's, the station-master's home, and just in time to rescue his little girl.

Mrs. Follet had heard the child's screams, for the tree was in the edge of the wood only a little way from the house, and she reached the place just after Steve had fallen to the ground, having seen the child's perilous position and Steve's rescue. She had dampened her handkerchief in a near-by spring and worked over the boy until consciousness returned.

The little white pinafore was soon running back with Mr. Follet walking rapidly.

"What under the cano*pee* does all this mean?" he asked excitedly as he came up, although Nancy had told him about the accident. "Are you hurt much, boy?" he went on.

Steve heard what was said in a vague way, but he couldn't reply and Mrs. Follet explained that she didn't think the boy was fully conscious yet, and they would have to try to get him to the house.

So Mr. Follet, who was a small but very wiry man, soon had him up in his arms, while Mrs. Follet supported his head and together they carried him to the house and laid him down on a couch. Then Mrs. Follet quickly fixed him a hot drink and gave it slowly to him. With each swallow the sturdy boy felt stronger, and by the time he had taken a cup full, was able to talk freely.

"Where under the cano*pee* did you come from anyway? You don't live hereabouts, do you?" asked Mr. Follet, who was of the restless, nervous temperament which must know things at once.

"Now, Pa," said Mrs. Follet, "you must get the doctor to set his arm before you ask him anything," and Mr. Follet started off.

Steve looked curiously at the arm hanging limply by his side. He had never seen a broken arm before though he had heard that arms and legs could break and be mended like hoe or ax handles.

By questioning, Mrs. Follet found that he had had nothing to eat since the day before, so she prepared him a dainty meal which filled the mountain boy with wonder. There was a poached egg, a bit of toast and a cup of hot milk, none of which had he ever tasted or seen prepared before. But it all was very, very good, and as he ate Nancy slipped shyly into the room. She had stayed outside in frightened misery, feeling that all the trouble was her fault. Her mother said kindly:

"That's right, child, come on in; our boy is better now." The little girl sat down timidly on the edge of a chair, and Steve took in the complete vision.

Soft yellow locks strayed out from a ribbon and tumbled about before a pair of deep blue eyes. Round cheeks were pink and soft, sweet lips were red and shyly smiling, a white apron with ruffles almost covered a blue gingham dress. The boy held his breath at the beauty of the apparition. He had never dreamed of anything so sweet and pretty in all the world.

It was not long before Mr. Follet returned with the doctor and the broken arm was successfully set, Steve bearing the pain "like a trump," as Mr. Follet put it. Then Mrs. Follet said he must go to bed at once, and he went up a tiny flight of stairs to a bed in a little attic chamber which she had made ready. Knowing the ways of mountain folk, Mrs. Follet did not insist that he undress, as the task would be difficult for him with the broken arm. He slept soundly in spite of pain in the arm upon a remarkable bed "off the floor" and awoke feeling well, and eager to see again his new friends.

When he got down the stairs, Mrs. Follet was busy getting the breakfast, and Mr. Follet was ready with questions.

"Where under the cano*pee* (which was a favourite expression with Mr. Follet) did you drap from yesterday, just in time to save our Nancy? You don't live hereabouts, do you?"

"No," said Steve, "I come from Hollow Hut."

"And where's that?" returned Mr. Follet.

Steve couldn't tell very clearly, but gave an account of his long journey and told about the watch and the fox skin which he was going to take to the man in the city.

Mr. and Mrs. Follet were much interested in his story, so much so that they forgot the waiting breakfast. Then they turned to it, but Steve had remembered that he dropped his fox skin as he ran to Nancy's rescue and he wanted to go at once for it, but Mrs. Follet would not let him go till he had eaten breakfast. The neatly laid table with its snowy cloth was a new wonder to Steve, and when the little girl, looking fresh and sweet as a rose, sat down opposite him, he was so awed and thrilled he could scarcely eat. Angels could hardly have given him a more heavenly vision than did this little girl.

Breakfast over, Steve started at once for the fox skin, and Mrs. Follet sent Nancy with him to help find it. The little girl lost some of her shyness as they looked for the skin, and Steve listened to her chatter, feeling in a strange way that it was all a dream which he had had before, as we do sometimes in experiences which move us strongly.

They found the skin with little trouble, and when they had carried it back to the house, Mr. Follet took it up and carefully examined it.

"So you're trying to get this here skin to the man in the city who sent the watch to you?"

"Yes," said Steve.

"And you ain't got hair or hide o' the watch now?" continued Mr. Follet.

"No, I hain't," said the boy sorrowfully.

"Well, I'll be sniggered," said Mr. Follet. "And how under the cano*pee* do you expect to find him in the city when you git thar?"

The boy's uncomprehending stare showed that he had no conception of a city, and Mr. Follet looked at his wife, laughed and went over to the station, which was station and store combined.

For a few days Steve continued to live in a dream. The house was a marvel to him. Mrs. Follet cooked on a stove and constantly fixed strange, nice things to eat; a clock ticked on the mantel, which comforted him somewhat for the loss of his watch,—there were queer but to him surprisingly beautiful and comfortable pieces of furniture, and one room had a nice piece of good stout cloth with red and green flowers on it spread over the floor on which people walked!

Then marvel of marvels, every now and then that engine and great train of cars came puffing and hissing by the house in full view, and the boy's spirits mounted on wings as he thought of the wonders of the world.

Even with one arm disabled, he took hold at once to help with the work about the place. He fed the chickens, horse and cow. With only one hand he could not learn to milk, though he was eager to do so. He went over to the store on errands and made himself useful in many ways.

One day when at the store he said to Mr. Follet that as soon as his arm was well he would have to be going on to the city to take the fox skin.

"And how under the cano*pee* do you expect to be ridin' round on the railroad without money?" said Mr. Follet. He knew well the boy had none. "You ain't a Rockefeller or a Jay Gould, air you?"

These allusions of course meant nothing to the boy, and the question of money was a new one to him. None of his late friends in their simplicity had thought of it, and the man had to make clear the need of it in the business world which Steve had come into. With his people things had always been "swapped"; corn, tobacco and whiskey, for the few things they needed from a store, and he had seen very few pieces of money in his life.

"Now, how under the cano*pee* are you going to come up with the money?" asked Mr. Follet briskly, and with practical pertinence.

Steve certainly did not know and then Mr. Follet proposed that he stay with them through the summer, work for him and he would give him his board and clothes and pay him fifty cents a week.

Steve agreed readily and at once felt a new sense of responsibility and manliness.

When his arm was quite well Mrs. Follet gave him some long white garments which she called "nightshirts," and told him to undress at night and wear them for sleeping! It was a very needless performance, he felt in his secret heart, but he had already learned to love the gentle woman and he would have done even more foolish things to please her. In fact, the thing which she gave him for brushing his hair seemed at first to bring him to the limit of acquiescence, but the bit of broken looking-glass stuck in one of the timbers of his room soon told him that a little smoothing down of his tousled head made an immense difference in his looks, and somehow made him seem a little more worthy to be in Nancy's presence.

The little girl had lessons at night from her mother in wonderful books, and Steve listened with rapt attention each time, beginning very soon to catch their meaning. It was not long till he had confided to Nancy how his "mammy" had wanted him to "larn things" too, and that was another reason why he was trying to get to the city.

"You're going to school then," said the little girl. "My mama teaches me, and some day she is going to send me to a big, big college."

Mrs. Follet had been a school-teacher from the north in one of the small Kentucky towns, an orphan girl, who very young had been obliged to make her own way in the world. She had met Mr. Follet, and in one of those strange attractions between complete opposites in temperament and training, had married him. She was a quiet, refined and very kind-hearted woman. She would gladly have taught the boy, but finding that he did not know even his letters, she felt that with Nancy in the second reader, she could not take another pupil who was a beginner.

But when the lessons were going on in the evening Steve soon began to spell over the words to himself as Nancy spelled them, and then it came about that often at odd times the brown shock of hair and the little yellow curls bent together over bits of paper, as the little girl pointed out and explained the make-up of the letters to the big boy.

"Don't you see, Steve, this little chicken coop with a piece across it is big A, and this one with the piece standing up and two curly things at the side is big B." The peculiarities of similar letters were discussed, how the bottom curly thing in big R turned the other way, while P didn't have any bottom curly thing at all, and F didn't have any bottom cross piece, while E did.

"See here," said Steve, growing alert, "here's a powerful nice gate; whut's that?"

"Oh, that's big H," said Nancy, "and wriggly, twisty S is just the prettiest letter of all, I think. Oh, Steve, that is the letter which begins your name," said she, in generous, childish joy.

"Is that so?" exclaimed Steve, with eager pleasure because she was pleased. "And which is the one whut begins yourn?"

- 30 -

"Oh, mine is just two straight standing up pieces with a slanting piece between. It's one kind of a gate but not just like H," and she hunted out an N to show him.

"I think that's the prettiest letter of all," said Steve, with unconscious gallantry. "Whar's the other letters in yo' name?" he inquired, and Nancy hunted them all out. Then she found the other letters in his name, and Steve had an undefined disappointment that his name did not have a single letter in it which belonged to her name. It seemed to shut him out more completely from the things which belonged to her.

So the lessons went on from the little girl to the big boy, and Mrs. Follet was amazed one day to find that Steve could read quite well. He studied every book and paper within reach as he found time, though he never neglected his duties.

Corn was constantly brought Mr. Follet in exchange for goods at the store, and one of Steve's duties was to take the old horse with two big bags of corn over to the Greely mill to be ground into meal. Nancy was mounted upon the old horse in front of the bags to show Steve the way on his first trip, and afterwards she always begged to go. To Steve it was the greatest joy to take the little girl with him, though he wouldn't have dared ask it. He taught her to put her small foot in his hand while he sturdily lifted her to the old white mare's back, and on the return she stepped down into his palm with equal ease.

The way to the mill lay along the road for a time, and then a short cut was made across what was known as the Greely Ridge. It was a steep cliff of rugged woodland, and both Nancy and Steve enjoyed the trip through the woods, Steve walking close beside the horse and the two chatting all the way. He told the little girl such interesting things about birds and squirrels, rabbits and foxes.

"Don't you wish we were birds," said Nancy one day, "so we could fly way off and see lots of things?"

"Yes," said Steve, "I shore do; then I could find Mr. Polk and give him his fox skin." The thought of getting to Mr. Polk was always in his mind, and though the little girl knew all about it she wanted to hear again how Steve got the skin and about that wonderful day in the woods when he met Mr. Polk, and the beautiful watch that the robbers took.

"When you find Mr. Polk and learn to make watches and things, like your mother wanted you to, you will make one just like yours for me, won't you, Steve?"

"Yes, I shore will," said Steve earnestly, never doubting that he would keep his promise.

There was nothing Steve would not attempt for her pleasure. He went to the tops of trees after some vacant bird nest or hanging flower, he chased rabbits and hunted squirrels that she might get a glimpse of them.

The Old Greely Mill

"Some day, Steve," said Nancy innocently, "let's build us a house and live here always; we do have such good times when we come to this wood."

Steve replied again, "Yes, I shore will," and neither dreamed what the wood was hiding for them to be revealed, far out in the veiled future.

When they reached the mill, Mr. and Mrs. Greely were always so glad to see them. They had no children of their own and they liked the straightforward, dependable boy, while the little girl with her sweet, shy ways, was always a delight. Mrs. Greely would often stop her spinning to get a little treat for them, which they would eat while the corn was being ground, and going to mill came to make four people happy each trip.

VI

AN UNEXPECTED MEETING

Mr. Follet was a man of unique business methods. He had no idea of orderliness, though he insisted he knew where everything was, and strenuously declined his wife's offers to go over to the store, or stores rather, and help him "straighten up." The stock had overflowed the floor of the original building and instead of putting in shelves to dispose of the stock conveniently, he built another and still another shanty to hold the overflow. But in spite of queer methods he was making money steadily. He kept each building securely locked, for he said he wouldn't have idle folks sitting around in his store. He went over to the station according to the railroad time schedule, though it was only a flag station and was seldom flagged, and whenever he saw a customer at the store door or on the way, he bustled over to unlock the door, stumble around in the dark, for there were no windows, and hunt out what they wanted.

Bacon, molasses, dress-goods, coffins and farm implements were on close terms of intimacy and whatever was wanted Mr. Follet could produce with amazing promptness.

Such methods, however, consumed a great deal of time on the path between his home and the store, and Steve filled an urgent need of the combined establishment.

One morning at breakfast in early autumn Mr. Follet was in a great flutter of excitement. A travelling auditor of the railroad was to be there for the day looking over his accounts and this not frequent event was a sore trial to both the station-master and the auditor. Each time Mr. Follet said to him nervously: "Now, you know I can't keep things like the road tells me to, and if things don't just come out even I'll make up whatever's lacking."

When the auditor, a big, broad-shouldered, kindly-faced gentleman arrived on this particular morning, and was seated for work, Mr. Follet made his usual statement.

"All right, Mr. Follet, all right," said the genial auditor, "we know you are straight as a string. Are you sure you've got all the ticket stubs?" he continued as Mr. Follet brought out some bits of pasteboard from a big bushel basket.

"Oh, yes, I'm sure," said Mr. Follet. "I don't let nobody in here but myself and so nothing is out of place." Then thinking a minute, he said, "Well now I do believe I stuck a few stubs in this tin pail." He looked, and sure enough there were a few more.

"And the bills of lading," said the auditor, "are these all?"

Mr. Follet pondered a moment and then brightening, exclaimed: "Why no, I stuck a few of them in one of these here coffins one day for safe keeping," and he stepped over to a grim pine coffin keeping company with a pile of gay bandanas, and brought forth another bunch of bills. But his foot caught in a coil of barbed wire as he started over to the auditor with them and it was at that moment that Steve came to the station door to get something and Mr. Follet called out, "Here, Steve, hand these over to the gentleman." The boy started to obey, but when he turned and faced the auditor he stood rooted to the floor, his face white and eyes staring.

"What ails you?" said Mr. Follet sharply, noticing him. The auditor looked quickly up also, and the boy found his voice.

"Samuel Polk," he said slowly.

The auditor smiled, and replied pleasantly, "That's my name, son, and where did you ever know me?"

"Ye sent me the watch," said the boy.

"Is that so!" exclaimed Mr. Polk. "So you are the boy I met in the woods! Well, this is marvellous, sure, that we should meet here. How did you ever get so far away from Hollow Hut?" he went on smiling.

The boy told him briefly, while Mr. Follet listened with lively interest. When the pitiful tale of the loss of the watch was told, Steve added sturdily:

"But I got yer fox skin in spite of 'em, an' I've been a-workin' to git to the city to give it ter ye."

"Working to take the skin to me when you have no watch," said the auditor, gently.

"Course," said the boy; "hit was yourn jes' the same," and the auditor reached out and drew the boy to him tenderly, thinking of all the hardship he had borne in the effort to be square and honest.

"You are the boy for me," he said with a glimmer in his eyes that made Steve feel queer, and he broke away, saying, "I'll go and brung ye the skin."

He was back as quickly as his sturdy legs could bring him, and laid the fox skin on Mr. Polk's knee. It was gravely accepted and admired, and then Steve returned to his work with all the earnestness he could summon after the excitement of this unexpected meeting.

When Mr. Follet and Mr. Polk came over to dinner the acquaintance of the two who had met that November day in the mountains was continued and Mr. Polk was greatly pleased to find that the boy was already "larnin'," and astonished at the progress which had been made during the summer. On the way back to the store he said to Mr. Follet:

"I've taken a great fancy to that boy; he ought to have a good education. I am all alone in the world and no good to anybody. If it's all square with you, I'll take that boy to the city with me this afternoon when I leave at four-thirty and put him in school somewhere."

Mr. Follet was amazed and he hated to give up the boy who had become so useful, but after a moment's thought, he said:

"I don't see as I have anything to say about it. He just stopped here on his way to you, and you've come to him. You'll have to take him if you want him, though I don't see how under the canopee we'll get along without him now."

"That is just like you, Follet, straight always," said the other warmly, and after a little the station-master went back to take the news to Steve. It startled them all and Mrs. Follet expressed her great regret in seeing the boy go, but she put his few little belongings in good order and prepared him to start off "clean and whole," as she expressed it. Nancy looked on wide-eyed, and Steve got ready like one in a dream. He wrapped his small bundle of clothes in the fox skin, which Mr. Polk had asked him to take care of, and went over to the station.

At four-thirty the train rushed up. Mr. Polk led Steve into a beautiful plush-seated car and placed the boy where he could have a last look at his friends, for Mr. and Mrs. Follet and Nancy stood on the platform.

It was Nancy who held his eyes till the last moment, little Nancy with two big tears dropping down her cheeks. Steve's throat ached unaccountably.

VII

A TRIP TO THE CITY

"Here we are," said Mr. Polk, as the train thundered into the station at Louisville. The ride of four hours had been a continued kaleidoscopic delight. Steve could not understand how it was that trees and houses went racing by the car windows and Mr. Polk had rare enjoyment in the boy's unsophisticated inquiry and comment.

Bringing this boy into the city was like giving sudden sight to a child who had lived its life in blindness. With keenest pleasure, Mr. Polk took him into a brilliantly lighted restaurant for supper and then afterwards up town by trolley into a large furnishing establishment, for it was Saturday night and the stores were open. There he fitted the little fellow out from top to toe according to his liking, the outfit including a shining German silver watch! The two attracted attention everywhere, the boy's face a study in its swiftly changing expression and the man full of eager interest which he could not curb.

When Steve was all dressed and stood before a mirror, Mr. Polk exclaimed:

"Now, that is something like!" And the boy turning from the transformed vision of himself, lifted a quivering face to his benefactor.

There was a delicately sensitive side to the nature of this boy of the woods. To him this experience was not simply getting new, fine clothes, but his old familiar self seemed to go with the old clothes, and like the chrysalis emerging into the butterfly, he could not pass into the new life, which the new type of clothes represented, without having his joy touched with the pain of travail.

With the tenderness of a woman Mr. Polk put his arm about the little fellow in quick contrition, knowing that it had been too much for this habitant of the quiet woods, and said in a most matter-of-fact way: "Now, son, for home and bed," and in a few minutes more the boy was snugly tucked in bed in Mr. Polk's comfortable bachelor quarters, and the next morning when he woke he was a new boy inwardly as well as outwardly.

He was ready for new "thrills" and they came. After a very astonishing breakfast he went with Mr. Polk to church. The beautiful building and wonderfully dressed people held his wide-eyed interest, but when the deep-toned organ poured forth its solemn melody, big tears dropped down the boy's face and Mr. Polk drew him within a protecting arm. It was like touching the quivering chords of a little bared soul with new, strange harmonies, and the sensitive heart of the man understood intuitively the boy's mingled joy and pain.

In the afternoon Mr. Polk took his charge to the home of a friend to see about schools, as his friend had a boy about the same age, and also to get help as to the general problem of caring for his protégé.

Arrived at the house, the friend, Mr. Colton, his wife and Maud, the young daughter about fifteen years of age, were at home and gave the visitors a lively welcome. They were at once greatly interested in the mountain boy, but so civilized was his outfit, and intelligent his face that they could not realize his difference from themselves except when he talked. This they were delighted to get him to do, and he answered all questions unabashed, though he liked better to look and listen.

The Coltons were well-to-do people with ever-ready, easy hospitality and insisted that Mr. Polk and Steve remain to tea.

"The maids are both out as it happens, so we must get tea ourselves," said Mrs. Colton, adding with mock graciousness, "and everybody may help!"

They all trooped out in responsive pleasantry through the hall, and Mr. Colton inquired:

"Where is Raymond?"

"Oh, he is out," replied Mrs. Colton. "There is no telling when he will be in."

That they were very indulgent parents and Raymond was an exceedingly lively boy, Mr. Polk already knew.

The hostess and her daughter exchanged glances of sudden consternation when they reached the dining-room, then burst into merriest laughter.

At last Mrs. Colton said between subsiding ripples, "Father, please go down in the basement and look in the furnace and you'll find the baker with the cold roast left from dinner! Mr. Polk, you go along too, please, and you'll see some loose bricks between the joists right under this dining-room window, and right behind them is the bread-box which you can bring up!"

"The cake is up-stairs in the hat-box of my trunk under lock and key," gaily put in Maud, "and you can come with me, Steve, and bring down the preserves from under the bed!"

By this time the whole family were in gales of laughter, and Steve was greatly puzzled at this new phase of civilization. Mrs. Colton finally explained that for a few Sundays past Raymond had been carrying off everything there was to eat in the house, and having "spreads" in the barn with his chums. This time they determined to outwit him.

Mr. Polk joined heartily in all the merriment, going after and bringing in provisions, but in his heart he thought, "This is the product of too much opportunity—give me my mountain boy every time. If he doesn't outstrip this pampered son, I miss my guess."

A little later Raymond came in and dominated the conversation at once, after the manner of too many bright, confident children of modern city life. After tea he took Steve in charge on a lively tour of exploration, and Mr. Polk talked over his plans for his boy.

"The thing you ought to do," said Mr. Colton who was very clear-headed concerning everything except his own son, "is to put the boy in a mountain college. He would be at a disadvantage among boys of his age in town, and then you've no way to take care of him, travelling as you do. My wife has a friend near here who is greatly interested in a mountain college; just go over and see her."

This seemed good advice and Mr. Colton took Mr. Polk and Steve over at once.

The lady came in and greeted them with gracious cordiality, but when she learned their errand and knew that one of the little mountain boys, to whose welfare she had given so much thought, time and money, was before her, her eyes grew tender and filled with tears.

"He must go to our mountain college at once; the school has just opened," she said. So they heard all about the school and its opportunities. When she had finished Steve spoke up:

"Is all that jes' fer mountain boys lack me?" This seemed beyond belief, but they assured him it was.

Raymond had greatly enjoyed demonstrating the mysteries of the telephone, electric lights and various contrivances of his own to so totally unenlightened and yet so appreciative an intelligence as Steve's, while the quaint mountain speech interested and amused him exceedingly. So when Mr. Polk and the boy took leave of the Coltons for the night Raymond secured a promise that Steve might attend school with him next day. Mr. Polk would be busy making arrangements for the few days' holiday which would be necessary to take Steve back to the mountains and place him in school.

- 38 -

Promptly next morning Raymond arrived at Mr. Polk's rooms for Steve and the boys started off together like two comrades. It was Steve's first day in a schoolroom, and eye and ear were on the alert, taking in everything.

He was well dressed and with his intelligent face the other boys noted nothing unusual until the noon hour when Raymond introduced his new specimen with keen relish. He had no unkind intentions in the sly winks he gave chosen comrades, but these aroused the curiosity of his fellows, and when Steve began to talk the boys awoke to lively possibilities. One after another began to ask questions.

"What did you do for fun down at Hollow Hut?" asked one.

"We uns didn't do nothin' fer fun, 'cep'in' hunt cotton tails, foxes an' coons," answered the boy.

"Didn't you play football?" asked some one else.

"I nuver hearn tell of it," said Steve.

"Du tell," returned another boy, venturing to fall a little into the stranger's vernacular.

"Didn't you ever play tennis, shinny or baseball?" persisted some one else, and Steve replied politely "that nobody ever hearn o' them things in Hollow Hut."

The boys then began to venture more boldly into imitations of Steve's speech while some got behind him and doubled up in silent laughter. Raymond looked on, feeling himself the hero of the day in having furnished such a comedy.

Suddenly Steve turned, perhaps with some intuition of what was going on, and with swift comprehension knew that he was being made fun of. His face on the instant was electrified with wrath. He drew himself up, and clenched his hands. Then in a twinkling his coat and cap were upon the ground. Taking the first boy at hand Steve dealt him a blow from the shoulder with a lean, sinewy arm that sent him spinning across the yard, and before any one could realize what was happening three or four others followed, and the rest, frightened at his fury, took to their heels with speed.

Steve stood alone at last quivering from head to foot; then calming slowly, he took his coat on his arm, put on his cap and walked away, not knowing whither he was going. But as he grew more quiet he took his bearings, and his keen sense of direction and good recollection of things they had passed in going, led him without trouble back to Mr. Polk's rooms.

Raymond was not a cad, and when he had time to think was thoroughly ashamed of himself. He went to the teacher and made confession; then as both were afraid the boy might get lost or come to some harm, he went at once on a search. He did not dream that Steve could so directly find his way back, and Raymond wandered about for hours in a fruitless search, doing without his dinner. At last, frightened and contrite, he went to Mr. Polk's office. Here the confession was harder to make, but it came out in all its humiliating details. Having eased his conscience he wound up with a burst of enthusiasm: "I tell you, Mr. Polk, Steve's got the stuff in him. There isn't a fellow in school but thinks he is fine. We didn't mean a thing by our fun, but he served us just right, and every fellow wants to take his paw."

Mr. Polk said little but sending Raymond home and promising to telephone later, he went directly to his rooms, knowing Steve's keenly intuitive mind better than Raymond. Though anxious until it was proven true, Mr. Polk found Steve as he had expected, seated in his rooms when he got there. But he saw a most dejected little figure. The new clothes were laid aside, the old mountain things were on, and the boy's face was drawn and white, though he fronted Mr. Polk sturdily.

"I don't belong in no town. I ain't got no town ways. I'll jes' go back to Hollow Hut and stay thar."

Mr. Polk put his arm about the boy and gently drew him to a seat. For some moments there was silence.

"Steve," he said at last, "did the trip over the mountains from Hollow Hut to Mr. Follet's sometimes seem hard for you?"

"Hit shore did," said the boy slowly.

"But you didn't give up the struggle, did you?"

"No," said Steve, still slowly.

"Well, the journey of life is like that journey over the mountains: it is often hard; there are things to overcome and things to endure. You have started now up the long, hard hill of learning, and I hope you are not going to turn back at the laughter of a few boys. You thrashed them out, I understand," he went on, and his voice held a strong hint of satisfaction; "pass right on now, putting the incident behind you just as you did each rocky summit you mounted on that difficult journey. You must climb to the top, son, understand; nothing short of that will satisfy me!" And he looked earnestly, almost vehemently into the boy's eyes.

The penetrating gaze was returned, but with a puzzled, groping inquiry for his benefactor's full intent.

"Yer mean I mus' larn as much as you know?" he asked at last.

"More,—infinitely more," said Mr. Polk with energy. "I have half-way climbed the mountain of knowledge and success in life,—I have even stopped less than half-way," he corrected a little bitterly, "but," rousing himself, "I want to begin life over again in you, and nothing but the very top of the mountain of success will ever satisfy me!" He turned again to the boy with a deep, searching gaze.

"You are a boy of your word," he went on after a moment, "that is what pleased me most about you, and now at the very outset of this business of learning and succeeding in life, I want your promise that you will not halt before obstacles, but go to the top!"

There was impelling enthusiasm as well as energy in the resonant tones, and Steve's spirit kindled with answering enthusiasm and a glimmering vision of heights which he had not hitherto glimpsed.

"I'll git ter the top, Mr. Polk,—ef I don't die on the way," he said with solemn earnestness.

It was a most unexpected, peculiarly intense moment for both, and in the silence which followed, the imagination of boy and man scaled lofty peaks, but the mountain of material success which filled Mr. Polk's vision was not the beautiful, mystic height upon which the boy gazed, and neither dreamed of the conflict which this fact was to bring about in future years.

"God hath set eternity in the heart of man," and the child of the woods felt the stirring of an eternal purpose, undefined though it was. The glamour of the world had long since intervened for the man.

The telephone rang noisily, having no respect for visions, and Mr. Polk rose to answer it while Steve began at once to put on again the new clothes in unconscious ratification of his solemn life-promise to Mr. Polk.

It was Mrs. Colton at the phone and she learned with great relief that Steve had been found. She insisted that Mr. Polk and the boy must come over to supper, after which there would be a little impromptu party of Raymond's friends for Steve.

The boy looked very sober when this announcement was made to him, but Mr. Polk smiled and said heartily, as he had already done to Mrs. Colton:

"Of course we will go!" And they went.

There was just a bit of awkwardness when the boys came into the Coltons' that evening and met Steve once more, but Mr. Polk, with an adroit question, started him to telling them about trapping rabbits, chasing foxes and treeing coons while the boys became so interested, including Steve himself, that all unpleasantness was forgotten. Upon leaving, each boy took Steve's hand with real respect and liking, and Raymond expressed the general sentiment when he exclaimed, "You're a brick!"

Next day Mr. Polk and Steve started for the mountain school. As they sat together on the train Steve said: "I'll be larnin' to do things jes' like mammy said fer me ter do. I wonder ef she will know."

"I think so," said Mr. Polk simply, but with a gentle sympathy in his voice, which, whenever expressed by look or tone, seemed to bring the boy close to the heart of the man. Resting a moment in this embrace, Steve asked a question which had come to him several times. His father and all the mature men he had known had been married,—for bachelors are rare in the mountains,—why had Mr. Polk no wife?

"Is ye woman dead, Mr. Polk?" was the question he asked.

"No," answered Mr. Polk, with a smile that flitted quickly, "she did not marry me at all, and so has left me lonely all my life. I would have been a far better man had she done so. As it is," and the bitterness crept into his voice again, "I stopped half-way up the hill of success as I told you, and threw my prospects away. That is why you are to live my life over for me and bring success whether or no."

VIII

OPPORTUNITY

Mr. Polk and Steve made their railroad trip by night, and the sleeper with its rows of shelf-like beds was a fresh experience for the boy, but he climbed to the upper berth and slept the sleep of healthy youth. They reached L—— about seven o'clock in the morning, and the sight of mountain and valley spread out before them in purple beauty gave a strange thrill of joy to Steve. The mountaineer's love of the mountains rushed upon him after all his new, pleasant experiences with a first consciously defined emotion.

"Well," said Mr. Polk, "now the problem is how we can cover that forty miles which lies between us and our school." But just at that moment he spied an old man helping a woman into a wagon, and at once he stepped up, found they were fortunately going to the same point, and would gladly take in two passengers with the ready accommodation of mountain people.

They travelled leisurely on and on, Steve seeing things of a familiar type and Mr. Polk much that was fresh and interesting. They stopped over night at a little settlement and journeyed on again next day, reaching their destination early in the evening. When the group of school buildings came into view, the old mountaineer pointed out the main building with its tower, and told them which was the "gals' sleepin' place," and which "the boys' sleepin' place," as he termed the two dormitories. He drove directly to the president's home, a little unpainted frame house. They were cordially received, entertained at supper and taken afterwards to the boys' dormitory, where Steve was given a room with several other boys. Then they walked over to "The Hall," as it was called, and were introduced to the teachers, who were gathering there for the study hour. They had met several when a young woman's trim, slender figure, with a decided air of the city about it, appeared in the doorway, and the light from within lit up a pair of clear, steady brown eyes, a pleasant mouth with firmness lurking in the corners, and fluffy brown hair put back in a roll from a very attractive face.

She stood a moment there in the doorway with a casual glance for the strangers, then suddenly caught her breath and went white, but instantly recovered herself as the president, oblivious of any tragic moment for her, turned and said:

"This is Miss Grace Trowbridge; she came down here all the way from New York City to teach mountain boys and girls,—and she knows how to do it, too."

Miss Trowbridge bowed and passed quickly within the hall.

- 43 -

Mr. Polk acknowledged the introduction with a look on his face that Steve had never seen before, and the boy felt somehow that his good friend had become a stranger as they walked back to the boys' dormitory for the night. Next morning, too, something had come between them, and when Mr. Polk said he would leave that day instead of staying several days, as he had intended, Steve could make no reply.

Before Mr. Polk left, however, in giving final instructions to his charge, the old kindly manner returned, and as he said, "I hope you will like it here, son," the boy replied with his old freedom:

"I knows I'm a-goin' to like it, and that thar Miss Grace Trowbridge is the nicest one of 'em all. She used ter live in New York City, the president said, whar you used ter live. Didn't you nuver know her thar?" he asked innocently, not yet comprehending in the least city conditions.

Mr. Polk set his lips grimly and answered sternly: "Yes," as he mounted a mule to ride back the forty miles to the nearest railroad station.

What was the matter again? The boy did not know, and he felt as though a sudden chill had come upon him. But a moment later Mr. Polk looked down at him kindly, reached over, pressed his hand, and said: "Be a good boy," as he rode away on the ambling mule.

So Steve began his school life. He went into the second reader class, his opportunities at the Follets' having put him beyond the beginners. In his class were children of all ages and mature men and women, who were just getting their first opportunity to learn. Steve was bright and quick, had a good mind, and made rapid progress.

With the superior social advantages which he had found along the way from Hollow Hut to the school, the boy became a great ally of the teachers in the battle for nightgowns, combs, and brushes for the hair and teeth, also for white shirts, collars and neckties on Sunday, which most of the boys thought "plum foolishness anyways."

"Here, fellows," Steve would say when he found them turning in at night with soiled feet, coats and trousers, "this ain't the way ter git ter be president." He organized a company of "regulators" in the boys' dormitory, and when any fellows turned in with soiled feet, coats and trousers, Steve's shrill whistle summoned the army and a lively pillow fight ensued which was hard on the pillows but always brought victory for nightgowns. And when a boy refused to brush his hair in the morning the regulators invariably caught him, and the penalty was a thorough brushing down of his rebellious locks by at least twenty-five sturdy young arms. Under such methods the cause of nightgowns and brushes was made to thrive.

There was another cause which was more difficult, but which enlisted all Steve's best endeavour. Mountain children are apt to know the taste of liquor from babyhood, but Steve had never liked it and neither had his mother. Occasionally parents, especially fathers, when they visited the school would bring the children bottles of "moonshine" to hide and drink from as they pleased, and the teachers found Steve a great helper, though his corps of "regulators" could not always be relied upon.

In the midst of his interesting, new surroundings Steve's mind often went back to the rock where Tige lay and to the grave of his "mammy." How pleased she would be, he thought again and again,—maybe she was—that he was where he could "larn things."

He soon began to write letters to Mr. Polk, and a steady improvement was noted all winter in these letters. There was always a great deal in them about Miss Grace, for she seemed to make him her special charge and the two were great friends. She loved to walk in the woods and talk with Steve, hearing him tell many interesting things which he had learned from intimate association with birds and animals. Sometimes she would take his hand at the top of a hill and together they would race down, laughing and breathless to the bottom. After such a run, one day, they halted by the bank of a stream beneath one of the grand old beeches for which Kentucky is famous.

"Oh, Steve," she exclaimed enthusiastically, "what a beautiful old beech this is. How symmetrical its giant trunk, how perfect its development of each branch and twig, while it pushes up into the sky higher than all its fellows, gets more sunshine than all the rest, has the prettiest growth of ferns and violets at its base,—and I just know the birds and squirrels love it best!"

Miss Grace had a bubbling, contagious enthusiasm, and Steve followed her expressive gestures as she pointed out each detail of perfection with answering admiration.

"Steve!" She turned suddenly and bent her eyes upon him with still more radiant emphasis. "I want you to be just such a grand specimen of a man! Big and strong and well developed,—pushing up into the sky further than all the rest about you, getting more sunshine than any one else—making little plants to grow and blossom all about you and drawing to you the sweetest and best in life!"

He smiled back into her shining eyes, somewhat bewildered, but with an earnest:

"I shore will try, Miss Grace, but I don't know just what you mean."

"I mean I want you to study hard, to develop every power of mind and body you have, and then,—give your life for the uplift of the children of the mountains."

She did not press him for a promise, nor linger upon the subject, but the first dim outline of that mystic height of the boy's vision had been traced.

Upon another walk which they took together Steve asked Miss Grace how she happened to come from her home way up in New York down to Kentucky to teach mountain boys and girls, and she was silent a moment, a look which he could not fathom coming over her bright face. At last she said, "I was very foolish; I threw away happiness. Then I heard of this work and came here that I might redeem my life by making it useful."

There was something about this boy of the mountains that made the telling of the simple truth the natural thing; but startled at even so vague a revealing of her bruised heart, she turned the talk quickly to other things.

IX

A STARTLING APPEARANCE

In the spring following came a great day for the mountain school when some friends and benefactors were coming. Great preparations were made. The school about three hundred strong fronted the main hall, and there was great waving of small and large handkerchiefs in a genuine salute as the visiting party drove up.

When the company had scattered a little after the greeting, Steve suddenly felt an arm about him and turning, found Mr. Polk smiling down upon him. The boy was overjoyed and could only cling to his hand, speechless for a moment. Mr. Polk had met the visiting party on the train, among whom was the lady who had told him of the school, and she would take no refusal,—he must go with them.

It was a beautiful day for Steve and in his boyish talk about his life and school he often spoke of Miss Grace, but each time came that grim setting of Mr. Polk's lips and the boy soon instinctively dropped her name. The day was destined to be full of events, some in honour of the visitors and some that were totally unexpected.

The speech of welcome from the school was made by Stephen Langly. Miss Grace had told him to say in his own words whatever was in his heart to say. So the boy stepped out from the gathered school, mounted a little platform and stood before the assembled crowd unabashed, for the mountaineer knows no embarrassment, while in simple good English he thanked the generous friends and teachers for what they were doing for mountain boys and girls. As he stood there well dressed, erect, manly, he bore little resemblance to the forlorn boy who had crept away from his cabin home at Hollow Hut a year before.

As the crowd dispersed a little after the speech-making, in which several took part, Mr. Polk and Steve walked away together and passed a group of teachers and students of which the visiting lady of Mr. Polk's acquaintance was the centre.

"Come here, Mr. Polk, please, and bring Steve to see me," she called.

Miss Grace Trowbridge was one of the group and Mr. Polk halted reluctantly, but finally joined them.

Before a word could be exchanged a tall, lank, grim mountaineer slouched forward and laid a horny hand upon Steve's shoulder. The startled boy looked up to see his father standing beside him!

The Kentucky mountain product, unlike any other so-called shiftless man in the world, may idle his days away with pipe and drink, but let a wrong, real or fancied, be done him or his and in his thirst for vengeance he is transformed. His energy, his perseverance, his intelligence, his fury become colossal. So, Jim Langly, convinced after months of waiting and brooding that his boy had been enticed away by the giver of the watch, had set out with a grim purpose of finding boy and man which had been undaunted by any obstacle. With slow but persistent effort he had traced the child over mountain and valley, often losing all clue, but never relaxing till at last he had reached Mr. Follet and learned that the boy was in school. From thence he easily made his way to the school of Mr. Polk's selection, and, arriving by strange providence upon a gala day, had found the two objects of his search at the same moment.

"I've found ye at last," he said grimly, "an' when I set eyes on the man whut give ye that watch and tolled my boy away from his home, I'll shoot him down lack a dog!"

Mr. Polk quietly walked out and said, "I am your man, Mr. Langly."

"You," the enraged mountaineer yelled, and jerking a pistol from his trousers pocket, he lifted and would have cocked it, but quick as a deer Grace Trowbridge had stepped in front of Mr. Polk, protecting him with her body, while Steve threw himself on his father and screamed shrilly, dropping into the speech of the mountains:

"No, oh, pappy, pappy, don't shoot him! He nuver got me ter leave home; I went myself, and I'll go back with yer and stay all my life!"

Frantically the boy clung to his father, pleading pitifully, while Grace Trowbridge with all her strength pushed Mr. Polk back among a quickly gathering crowd. Others joined her, and in the excitement of the moment, both she and Mr. Polk were hurried into safety within one of the school buildings and the door locked upon them.

The town constable was on the ground, for his services were quite likely to be needed in any public gathering, and before Jim Langly realized what was happening, being wholly unfamiliar with the ways of law and order, his pistol had been wrenched from his hand (something unheard of in mountain ethics), and he was hurried from the scene like an infuriated lion made captive.

Breathless and spent, Grace Trowbridge found herself looking into the face of her old lover when the door was locked upon them. She stood an instant like a frightened bird driven to cover, her eyes gazing into his, anxiety, relief, tragic intensity born of but one emotion in her white quivering face,—and then the warm blood surged up with returning realization of the years of estrangement between them, and she wheeled for instant flight.

But the door was locked, and baffled she faced him again, crying, "Oh, Sam, let me out!"

For answer he caught her in his arms and said, "Let you out, and away from me? Never! I shall hold you fast instead. I love you, love you, love you," he cried vehemently, "and what is more, you love me!" He crushed her to him and the tense, spent figure relaxed in his arms while love in full tide swept over them, after six weary years of longing and restraint. Their separation had followed a misunderstanding which now did not even seem to need explanation.

"Sam," she cried at last, moving energetically away from him, "I can never give up these blessed mountain children. You'll have to adopt every one of them if you take me!"

"All right," he said happily, "just as many of them as you please."

Instantly both remembered Steve.

"Oh, Sam, where is Steve? Do you suppose his father has carried him off, and that we will never see him again?" she exclaimed in distress, and a few moments later, when release came to them, their first anxious inquiry was for the boy.

No one had seen or thought of him in the excitement, and when the story of Jim Langly's arrest had been told them, they searched the grounds and buildings in great anxiety before they finally found Steve in his room.

When Mr. Polk opened the door the boy stood before him dressed in a little ragged shirt and old pair of trousers he had worn for hunting and with bared feet. The hopeless expression of the lost was in his face.

"I can't keep my promise to you, Mr. Polk," he said brokenly. "I can't ever climb that mountain fer yer, but it is better fer me ter die on the way than fer you to be killed." Correct speech had no part in such despair.

Mr. Polk drew the boy to him while Miss Grace stood without, her lips tremulous and eyes full of tears. After a silent moment Mr. Polk led the boy outside and put him in her arms.

"Do you think we are going to give you up?" Mr. Polk said, striding up and down the hall. "Not by a long shot," he went on with energy, and a conviction for which he could not at the moment see any tangible foundation. "This is all going to be fixed up,—just leave everything to Miss Grace and me."

The boy shook his head. "Ye don't know pappy," he said sadly.

"I may not," returned Mr. Polk cheerfully, "but I know Grace Trowbridge, and I am going to trust her to keep you here. Do just as she says, son, and everything will come right."

He left them to talk with the president of the school. They discussed what should be done with Jim Langly. Mr. Polk greatly regretted the man's arrest, but was compelled to admit it could not have been avoided. He begged, however, that prosecution of the case be delayed until every effort could be made to make Langly see that only good was intended for his son.

"Of course I must relinquish all claim to the boy," he said sadly, "but we must by some means win the father's consent that Steve remain here,—that is the important thing."

So it was decided that Mr. Polk should leave, as his presence could only infuriate the man, and the president gladly promised to do everything in his power to win the father.

For a week Jim Langly remained in the lock-up of the town. He had wrenched his back severely in the struggle with his captors; then, like a caged lion indeed, he had beaten the walls of his prison all night without food or drink, and being a man of indolent habits, he collapsed utterly next morning. The gaunt, haggard face with deep hollows beneath the eyes, the giant figure lying helpless upon a rude couch of the lock-up touched deeply the heart of Grace Trowbridge when she went in to see him. In his blind fury he had not noticed her especially the day before; and when, without saying a word, she stepped lightly across the room and reaching through the iron bars closed a rude shutter to screen the glare of the morning sun from his eyes, then gently adjusted a pillow beneath his head and fed him a cup of hot broth, he accepted it all like a wild, sick animal which in its helplessness has lost all animosity to man.

During the day she tended him unobtrusively, but with infinite kindness, and next morning she found him better, but still willing to accept her care. He even watched her with a far-away interest as one would something unknown and yet strangely pleasing. By the third morning she talked to him a bit as she smoothed his pillow, and smiled as he ate her toast with relish.

At last he said with an effort, "Whar's Steve?"

"He is here," she said gladly, "just waiting outside the door for you to ask for him. He has been there every day," she added softly.

Then she stepped to the door and motioned for Steve. The boy came in, still dressed in mountain fashion, for no amount of persuasion could induce him to again put on the better clothes. This evidently met the father's approval, for a look of bitter expectancy which had come into his face faded at once as he saw the old trousers and bare feet.

"Set down," he commanded feebly, but not unkindly, though he had nothing more to say.

The two stayed with him through the day, and gradually Grace, with consummate tact, made conversation which included the three, though Langly took little part. Then she read a stirring story which compelled his attention and interest even though he had never heard anything read aloud before. It was the first time in the mountaineer's long life that he had ever been unable to rise from his bed and go his way and the helplessness had softened his spirit like the touch of a fairy's wand. As he listened to the sweet, cultured voice of the woman while she read and saw Steve with quickened intelligence following every word, he realized for the first time that the world held strange things in which he had no part, but for which his boy was ready.

At last Miss Grace turned to Steve and said in the most natural manner, "My throat is getting tired; won't you read a little for us?"

The boy looked at his father in quick alarm, but the gaunt face betrayed nothing, and the reading went on in Steve's boyish voice.

Several days passed during which Miss Grace and Steve had been constantly with the prisoner, then his injured back was sufficiently restored to permit of his being raised in bed to a sitting posture, and Miss Grace felt it was time she tried to win his consent to Steve's remaining at school. With woman's intuition she divined the best method of approach. Steve was not there and she told with simple pathos of the boy's love for his mother. Jim Langly had loved his wife with all the mountain man's lack of expression, but the natural portrayal of the boy's affection did not displease him. The old self in fact seemed to pass out with that day of terrible fury and the softer spirit which had taken its place seemed to linger. She went on to tell how the boy's mother had longed for him to have a chance to learn, and that only a few minutes before her death she had made him promise to go where he could learn.

"It was this," she ended, "which made Steve leave home and not the man who sent the watch."

Jim Langly lay silent a long while after hearing this, and then he said:

"I was agin that in her alive, I reckon I won't be agin her dead."

- 51 -

After a little he inquired with resentment in his voice, "How come that man whut give him the watch ter be with him here?"

"The boy happened to find the man," she said, "and the man was good to him when he needed a friend. But we will get Steve to tell us all about it," she ended brightly, as Steve came just then to the door. And with a glad heart the boy told all his story from the day he left Hollow Hut till his father's appearance a few days before.

The president of the school then visited Langly, told of the boy's progress and begged earnestly that he be allowed to stay. Nothing was said as to how the boy's expenses were to be met, and since Jim Langly knew as little as a child about the cost of such things, he asked no questions. When strong enough at last Langly walked out a free man, the president having withdrawn all charges against him, and after looking about the buildings with strange interest he started back to Hollow Hut, with no good-bye for his boy after the manner of the mountains, but with an understanding that when school closed Steve should return to his old home for the summer.

It was some two months later when Mr. Polk carried out this promise which had been made the father, by taking the boy back to the woods where they had first met. He expected to camp there for a few days' fishing, and to arrange for Steve's safe return to the school in the fall, as happy plans of his own for the autumn would probably prevent his coming in person.

When Steve left Mr. Polk he swung off down the well-remembered mountainside with strange joy in his heart. He had felt a new kinship for his father growing upon him since he could remain at school in the freedom of parental consent, and shy thought had come of reading aloud sometimes in the old Hollow Hut cabin from the pile of books under his arms while his father smoked and listened, as he had in the beautiful days when Miss Grace had tended him.

But a few hours later he came slowly back up the same path with a stricken look on his face.

"Pappy's dead, too," he said brokenly, when Mr. Polk stepped forward in surprise and alarm to meet him.

The boy sat down upon a log, dropping his books in a heap beside him, and his bent shoulders shook with sobs.

Mr. Polk comforted him with silent tenderness for a time, then gradually drew out the story of Jim Langly's short illness of a week from a virulent fever and his burial two days before.

Together they went again next day to the cabin. Mirandy had married a few weeks previous and she and her husband were beginning family life anew in

- 52 -

the old place. She had been stirred somewhat by the events of the year, and looked with interest upon Mr. Polk and Steve, the latter showing plainly to her the touch of new surroundings, and when Mr. Polk told her he wanted to take the boy for his own and educate him, she said with a touch of bitterness:

"Tek him erlong; he won't nuver know nothin' here."

So the two who had seemed bound from the first by close ties went away together, Steve to spend the summer at the school, where a few were always accommodated during the vacation, and Mr. Polk to wind up his business affairs in the South preparatory to a return to New York. He had formerly been associated with an uncle having large railroad interests in the East, who had often urged his return. He now proposed to do so, taking advantage of opportunities still open to him. These had been thrown away upon the breaking of his engagement with Grace Trowbridge, six years before, to take a position with a southern railroad and wander restlessly among new scenes.

X

STEVE DEVELOPS A MIND OF HIS OWN

In the autumn Mr. Polk's happy plans materialized. There was a wedding in a handsome New York City home, and Steve Langly arrived the day before for the festivities. At the ceremony he and Anita Trowbridge, the little sister of Miss Grace, were the attendants. They came in first, Steve dressed as a page in a velvet suit which went well with his clear, dark complexion, and little Nita, as she was called, tripped beside him in delicate pink as a fairy flower girl. They stood on either side of a beautiful fox-skin rug with a history, upon which the bride and groom, slowly following, took their places to repeat the sacred vows which bound them for life.

Steve and Nita, as the only children, spent the evening together, roaming about the house, Steve finding new interests everywhere. He looked around at the rich furnishings and beautiful floral decorations with appreciative eyes, seeming not at all out of place in such surroundings. A feeling of awkwardness and timidity might have possessed so poor a boy reared anywhere else, but mountain-born as he was, he accepted man's magnificence with the same tranquil spirit that he did the shimmering silver of a mountain sunrise or the gorgeous colour-triumph of its sunset. But he did not understand Nita. She tried her most grown-up ways upon him, chatting after the manner of a little society belle, and while she was so pretty that he loved to look at her as he would have looked at a beautiful flower, he did not know what to say to her. Having talked of many things, and being an ardent little lover of pretty clothes, taken in with appreciative eyes the handsome costumes of the guests, she sighed at last and said:

"Oh, I just love to go down Broadway, don't you, and see all the handsome gowns on people as they pass, and look in at the store windows!"

"I don't know; I nuver was there," he answered with a touch of his mountain speech, and then she laughed a silvery, childish laugh and said:

"You funny mountain boy," in a natural, frank way that made Steve smile back and feel more at ease.

After this they got on well as a couple of children, while Nita often exclaimed, "You funny mountain boy."

Mr. and Mrs. Polk called him their boy with a new sense of parentage after their marriage, and wanted to make him legally their son, but when it was proposed that he be known in the future as Stephen Polk, he looked far off into space a moment, and then as though his spirit had winged its way back into the wilderness of its birth, he dropped into the old manner of speech and said:

"I thank yer, but I was born Langly, an' I think I ought ter die Langly."

They said no more, and soon decided to send him back to the mountain school for his preparatory work at least, largely because Mrs. Polk was strongly convinced this was best for the boy; so, during the next six years, he spent the school terms in the mountains and his vacations in the north with his foster-parents. The last two summers he took work in a city university with special courses in geology and mining engineering, for Mr. Polk, knowing the rich treasures stored in the Kentucky mountains, had brilliant plans for Steve's future, dreaming of a time when the boy should be able to link these treasures with northern capital.

Mrs. Polk's dreams were of another sort altogether. She never lost interest in the cause of education in these same Kentucky mountains, and many were the talks she and Steve had about the progress being made there and the needs constantly developing. Engrossed in business, as Mr. Polk came more and more to be, he took no note of his wife's indirect influence, while she did not realize that she was interfering with plans of his.

As Steve grew to young manhood Mr. Polk asked him as often as studies would permit in summer to go down to the office. He liked to give the boy a taste of the financial whirl, and it was intensely interesting and exciting to Steve. He felt something of the same tremor of wonder and delight over the inner whirl of gigantic machinery moving railroad systems which stirred him when he felt the first rush of a passing railroad train, and there was a certain eager desire to be a part of it all.

It was upon his sixth vacation visit that Mr. Polk turned to him one day at the office as the boy's eyes glistened with interest and said:

"I shall want you at my elbow in a few years now. I shall be too old after a while to do all the things waiting to be done, and you remember your promise to climb that mountain of success for me whose heights I never shall be able to reach."

But the youth of nineteen suddenly looked afar as the boy of thirteen had done when it was proposed that he change the old name of Langly, and a vision of rugged mountains and deep valleys which again spread out before him were tracked by eager bared feet of poorly clad children hurrying towards the few schools which here and there dotted the wilderness. He was silent, for a definite conflict had begun in his soul.

Mr. Polk noticed the silence, and with a restless energy which was growing upon him, said to his wife that evening when they were alone:

"Look here, Grace, I am uncertain about Steve. That boy's unfathomable. Here I have been counting upon his going into business, and I know business appeals to him for I can see it in his eye, and yet when I spoke to him definitely to-day he just looked off into space," he ended in disgust.

Mrs. Polk laughed. "Well, you know, I have never been an enthusiast over money-making, and I don't believe Steve ever will be,—though he may."

"Why, look here," her husband said impatiently, "if he gets a good knowledge of geology and mining engineering, as I mean he shall, he can locate and open up some good mines in those Kentucky mountains which will make us all rich."

"Oh," laughed Mrs. Polk again, "that doesn't stir me a bit. But when I think of every little yearning child of the mountains well shod, with a clean kerchief in its pocket, and trudging away to school frosty mornings, then I begin to thrill."

"Of course," said Mr. Polk with impatient energy; "but money will help bring that to pass."

"Yes, but it isn't money alone that is necessary. They need an apostle of education, one of their very own who shall go among them opening their eyes to the world of knowledge and opportunity."

"And you would like our Steve to be that apostle, as you call him, I suppose." Looking at her intently a moment, he softened and added, "Well, you are a dear, unworldly woman." Then in sudden justification of himself, he went on: "I am willing he should be an apostle too, but one with money, so he can bring things to pass."

And he said no more to his wife, neither did he trouble Steve in the least with definite propositions for the future, but in the late summer of that year he remarked in a matter-of-fact way:

"Well, Steve, it must be college now for the next two years at least."

Whereupon Steve looked very sober and finally said: "Mr. Polk, you have been so good to me I cannot even talk about it. I do want to go to college more than I can express, but great, strapping fellow that I am, I ought not to accept your generosity any longer."

"Now, son," said Mr. Polk, with the tenderness he had given the little boy years before, "I want to do for you as I would for my own."

Steve said huskily, "I appreciate it deeply, but you know I couldn't give up my name, and it is just as hard for me to give up my independence. If I go to college at your expense it must be with the distinct understanding that I am to repay every penny spent for me. Forgive me," he added with a smile, "I suppose it is my mountain blood that makes me want to be free."

Mr. Polk, looking at the strong young face, knew that he must yield, and so the money was advanced for Steve's college expenses with the understanding that it was a loan.

The two college years were busy and profitable ones for Steve. He was fond of study and the regular courses of the school led him into new lines of interest while he still pursued his specialties of geology and mining engineering. The companionship of young men and women of inherited culture and opportunity of the best type was broadening and a fine means of general culture for him. Among the young women with whom he was thrown there developed no special interest for him, though he often wondered why. He, however, came to smile as he questioned his own heart or was questioned by chums, while he said, "We of mountain blood are slow, you know," and he failed to note how certain memories of soft yellow curls above a little white pinafore were so sacred that he never mentioned them.

He matured greatly in the two years, and at twenty-one was broad-shouldered from college athletics, six feet two in height, and his abundant dark hair with a suggestion of curl at the ends crowned a fine, clean-cut, somewhat slender face which in repose was serious, but possessed of a hidden smile which had formed the habit of flashing out suddenly, transforming his face with a peculiar radiance.

For the Christmas holidays of his last year at college he went home to the Polks as usual and one evening sat at the opera beside Nita Trowbridge in a little family party which included her. During all his comings and goings of the school years he had seen Nita with almost the familiarity of a brother. She was the child of middle age, petted and spoiled and much of a society butterfly as she developed into young ladyhood, though a very lovable one. Mr. and Mrs. Polk were greatly attached to her, and though it had not been hinted at, Steve knew that Mr. Polk would like nothing better than that they should marry when he was established in business. How Mrs. Polk would feel about it he was not so sure. Perhaps she doubted their congeniality of tastes.

As Nita sat beside him on this evening she watched Steve's rapt enjoyment of Wagner's beautiful, weird melodies. Between acts she said:

"How intensely you enjoy music!"

"Yes," he returned, throwing off the spell with an effort, "I do." And then with a reminiscent flash the smile broke over his face. "I remember well where I heard the first music of my life. It was when I was twelve years old, and from a mountain fellow who had had no training. But he simply made the banjo talk, as the darkeys would say, and reproduced with skillful touch and thrilling voice a fox hunt which fairly set me crazy.

"Then the next," he went on, "was at a church, just a little later, and never will I forget how the deep-toned organ stirred my soul to the very depths." There was a quiet solemnity upon him as he said this which Nita did not break for a moment. Then she said:

"How barren the mountains must be! You will never want to go there again, will you?"

"Barren!" he exclaimed in return. "I wish I were an artist in word painting and I would make mountain peak after mountain peak glow with rhododendron and laurel, fill the valleys with silver sunrise-mist to glorify their verdure for you, and then call out all the fur and feathered folk and troops of mountain children from their forest homes. You would not think it a barren country," he concluded with smiling eloquence.

"Perhaps not," she said slowly, "but to think of no good music, no pleasures, no,—anything that makes up our delightful living here," she ended.

"That is true," he responded gravely, adding almost to himself, "but it must be carried to them through work and sacrifice by somebody."

Then becoming conscious the next instant of the brilliant scene about him his smile flashed over his face again and he turned to her with:

"By the way, did you see an account in the papers of the wreckage of a car load of millinery in the Kentucky mountains a few days ago?"

"No, I did not," she smiled back.

"Well, there was a railroad wreck somewhere up there and a whole car load of millinery was sent out upon the four winds of heaven. Big hats and little, such as women know all about and men can't even talk of, with all sorts of gorgeous flower trimmings, feathers and ribbons were scattered through the woods, and they say barefooted mountain women flocked from every direction and decked themselves in the latest styles of head-gear."

Both laughed over the picture and Steve added:

"I suppose it would only need a procession of fashionable gowns parading the mountains to transform our women, while the sight of swallow-tails and silk hats might do as much for the men, for like the rest of the world we take up the superficial with ease, but"—sobering again—"to give our people a glimpse into the knowledge contained in books, to waken us to life's highest harmonies and open our eyes to nature's beautiful hidden colours, is going to take a long time, and as I said, somebody must work and sacrifice for it."

He searched the beautiful face beside him for sympathetic understanding, but she only looked at him with wide eyes as the frivolous little girl had done years before, not comprehending, while she wanted to say again, this time a little wistfully, "You funny mountain boy."

No conception of life translated into labour and sacrifice for others, such as he had begun to battle with, had ever come within her range of thought, and the starting of the music again was welcome to them both.

At the end of two years Steve was graduated, having been thoroughly prepared upon entering college, and when he returned to his foster-parents at the close of school they were greatly pleased with their boy. On the second night after his arrival Mr. Polk sat with him after dinner and smoked in great satisfaction. But it was of short duration. Steve had had a letter from his alma mater, the Kentucky mountain school, asking him to return as a teacher there the next year, putting forth strongly the need and opportunity for good. He had waited to talk the matter over with Mr. and Mrs. Polk before deciding, though it was pretty well settled in his own mind. He handed the letter to Mr. Polk.

"Of course you will not go," said Mr. Polk, with decision, as soon as he had finished it. "There is an opening for you in the office and I am anxious for you to take hold at once."

Steve looked afar again, as he had twice before when his fate was about to be settled for him, and Mr. Polk stirred impatiently. But the younger man turned at once, this time with that sudden smile upon his face, and said ingratiatingly:

"Mr. Polk, I am afraid I haven't any head for business,—I love books far better. I feel a premonition that I shall be stupid in business."

"Nonsense," said Mr. Polk, with quick irritation. "I don't believe it. You have never been stupid about anything."

"I do not know," Steve replied, serious again. "I have not been tried, I admit, and I must confess that business had a certain fascination for me as I have watched things stir in your office."

"Of course, of course," broke in Mr. Polk. "I have seen it in your face."

"But——" said Steve as promptly, and with a compelling earnestness in his voice that made the older man hold himself in restraint. "Mr. Polk, I must tell you something before we go any further in this matter. My barren boyhood has never faded from my mind. I cannot put it from me. I live it again in the thought of every little child hidden away in the mountains in ignorance and squalor.

"There may be little ones of my own blood in the Hollow Hut home," he added, and his voice dropped into a deep intensity which held them both motionless for a moment; then, for relief, breaking it again with that smile, he said: "I suppose it is the survival of our feudal mountain blood in me which makes me ready to go back to fight, bleed and die for my own."

"It is simply a Quixotic idea you have gotten into your head that you should go back to the mountains and spend your life trying to help your people," Mr. Polk replied emphatically.

"I don't deny you may be right," said Steve patiently, "but I got the idea fixed when I was a boy there at school having privileges which were denied so many, and you know one is very impressionable in early youth, and I confess that though for many pleasant reasons I have wanted to shake it off, I have been unable to do so."

This roused Mr. Polk to instant combat. He rose and strode the floor.

Mrs. Polk stood in the doorway an instant just then, but wisely and noiselessly slipped away.

"That's all right to want to help your own, but the practical way to do it is with money," he said vehemently.

"I am not entirely sure," returned Steve slowly. "I confess I may be mistaken—but I have thought and thought over this ever since you first proposed two years ago that I should go into business with you, and though, as I have said, I am still uncertain, I believe I ought to go there and work for my people. It will be ten years at least before I can do much in a monetary way, but I can begin teaching at once. Besides," he hurried on before Mr. Polk could speak, "people there need indoctrination,—inoculating so to speak, with the idea of education as much as they need money, and no one can do this so well as one of their own. Thanks to you, the best friend any boy ever had," he went on, his voice breaking a little, "I have had advantages which have fallen to the lot of few mountain boys, and I feel that my responsibility is tremendous."

- 60 -

"Yes," said Mr. Polk, "but I do not agree with you as to the best way of meeting it. However," he ended hotly, "I see you are like most young men of to-day whatever their obligations, you do not wish advice."

Steve was deeply hurt. "Mr. Polk," he said, "I would rather give my right arm than have anything come between us. If it were a matter of personal ambition, I would yield at once to your good judgment, but—please understand,—let me make this clear,—I am not sure that going myself to work among my people is the best way, but I simply feel it should be tried first. If I should remain here a while, I know I would never go there, and if I find that I am wrong in going, at the end of two years I will gladly return to you for business."

"If you go, Steve Langly, contrary to my advice and better judgment, you go for good," said Mr. Polk sternly, pausing in his striding and emphasizing with a stamp of his foot.

Mr. Polk with his gentleness had always had a hot-headed, unreasonable side to his nature. It was seldom in evidence, but it had shown itself years before in his break with his sweetheart and it was showing itself again with the boy whom he loved most devotedly.

Steve bowed his head in silent, dignified acceptance. Following a forceful law of human nature this unreasonable resistance (as he saw it) was fixing him very firmly in his own resolution. But the thought of all the older man had been to him rushed upon him again with softening effect, and he said sadly at last:

"I do not know how to make you understand, Mr. Polk,—but this need to go back to my own and try to help them is something inborn."

"I am afraid it is," said Mr. Polk curtly. "It is the mountain shiftlessness in you."

Steve rose with flashing eyes and heaving breast, but remembering again, he controlled himself, and sat down. His voice was cool and crisp, however, as he said a moment later:

"I have no intention of forgetting my debt to you, Mr. Polk, and you have a right to know what are my prospects for paying it." He named his salary, which was very meagre, and then added, "But my wants will be few,—and I have found that my pen promises to be a pretty good earning implement." This he added with reluctance, for he had not meant to tell it. "I shall pay you as soon as possible," he ended.

"Just as you please," said Mr. Polk again curtly, and strode this time out of the room for the night.

Steve soon followed, going to his room with a sense of desolation that was akin to the desolation of his boyhood in the wilderness. He felt that he must leave New York at once, for he could not stay longer with self-respect under the roof which had been home to him for so many years. What "little mother," as he had come to call Mrs. Polk, would say he did not know, but his heart warmed when he thought of her, and comforted at last by the feeling that she at least would not misunderstand him, he fell asleep towards morning. And in his fitful dreaming her sweet face was strangely crowned with soft yellow curls and she wore a little white pinafore!

The next day Steve had a long talk with Mrs. Polk. She had heard of the trouble from Mr. Polk, and had done all in her power to bring about a change in his state of mind. Failing utterly and knowing his tenacity when an idea was once fixed, she could not encourage Steve with the hope of any immediate change. Neither could she urge the young man to abandon his purpose, for she felt that he alone must decide his future, and though in her heart she approved his course, so deeply was she grieved over the alienation between him and Mr. Polk that she held it in restraint. She knew that she had helped to shape his determination, and woman-like was fearful now she had made a mistake.

When Steve said that he must go, she did not try to keep him, but her eyes were brimming with tears when he tenderly kissed her good-bye, as he had always been in the habit of doing, and she pressed a roll of money in his hand, whispering, "It is my own."

"No, no, little mother," he said with determined good cheer, "I do not need it. I was very economical the last few weeks at school, for I had forebodings of trouble; then,—I earned some money writing little stories for boys, the past year."

Scarcely noticing the last remark she hesitated a moment, wanting to insist that he take it, and yet reluctant. Then she held him by the shoulders with her slender hands, and said earnestly:

"If you ever need, you will let me know, will you not?"

"I certainly will, dearest little mother in the world," he said, his own eyes glistening with tears.

There was a formal leave-taking with Mr. Polk at the office, and then he went his way back to the mountains of his birth.

XI

EXPERIENCE

As the train carrying Steve southward reached a point where rugged peaks began pushing majestically up into the distant firmament he felt again the old thrill of the mountaineer's love of the mountains, while his trained eye noted with keen pleasure new details of line and colour. Then, when the railroad trip was over and he neared the end of the forty-mile wagon ride, bringing the little tower surmounting "The Hall" of his alma mater in sight once more, his face lit up with tender joy, for the old place had meant more to him than schools do to the average boy. Sweeping his eye back over a landscape where purple heights were tipped with sunset gold in the distance, giant beeches held aloft their summer leafage in the valleys and mountain flower-favourites bloomed in glorious June profusion everywhere, he inwardly exclaimed, with sudden reverence:

"That is God's part, the fashioning of this beautiful setting," and then turning again to the group of school buildings, "and this is man's,—the bringing of humanity into harmony with the perfection of His handiwork."

He had been unable to throw off entirely the depression which had followed the rupture with Mr. Polk, and deeply stirred emotionally as he had been in parting with Mrs. Polk, it required this spiritual interpretation of school life to restore his equilibrium.

But the battle involved in the step he had taken was by no means fought in that one flash of high conception. Being a wholesome, normal fellow with an ordinary amount of selfish desire for comfort (though he had seemed to follow a Quixotic idea into the wilderness), he found himself at once missing the luxuries of life to which he had become accustomed. All through the summer he travelled about on horseback,—sometimes on foot,—stopping often at little squalid cabins, and often also at meagre homes where housewives wrung his heart with their pathetic effort to be thrifty and cleanly on almost nothing, and everywhere he tried to inoculate the people with the idea of education. On the whole his experience proved more of a hardship than he had believed possible with his early mountain bringing up. He discovered that he had a decided liking for individual towels, and was quite capable of annoyance when obliged to bathe his face in a family tin wash-pan,—or temporarily idle skillet where wash-pans were unknown,—while his predilection for a bath tub with hot and cold water on tap had become more fixed than he had suspected.

"Have I already grown too fastidious to be helpful to my own people?" he asked himself in disgust. Then he squared his shoulders and set his lips in fresh determination. But, a moment later, with that sudden smile upon his face, he also resolved to compromise a bit with hardship. He stopped at the first wayside store and invested in towels which he learned to wash and dry at convenient times. This gave him pleasant independence, and since his bedroom had always been fixed in the open,—for from the first he could not bring himself to sleep in crowded rooms where whole families took their rest,—he could make his morning toilet without offense to his hosts, while a soapy plunge in some mountain stream became a luxury he would not readily forego. And always, whatever the hardship, there was the compensation of barefooted boys and girls held spellbound, and often fathers and mothers as well, while he unfolded the wonders of a world which lay beyond the mountain's rim, and always he had the advantage of being able to assure them that he, too, was mountain bred.

So, with contending against many things distasteful on one side, and exhilaration while little hands clung to his as his had clung to Mr. Polk's that long ago day in the heights about Hollow Hut, the summer passed and he began his work as teacher.

He had long known that he would enjoy teaching, and took up his duties with keen interest. Fortunately for him he had little conceit or pedantry, which would have been a fatal handicap for him as teacher among his own people, simple-hearted though they were. He organized his work with straightforward earnestness and quiet ability and things usually moved smoothly in his class room. But many old difficulties in the life of the school with which he had seen the teachers battling when he was a pupil promptly presented themselves afresh to test the tact, skill and wisdom of the young teacher. Some boys still came to school with well-developed taste for tobacco and liquor which parents still indulged, and passing mountaineers often good-naturedly fostered. Having helped to battle with these things as a boy he knew somewhat how to handle them. But another matter of which he took little note in his student days, but which had nevertheless always been a difficult problem, was love-making in the school. He was sorely puzzled how to wisely handle this.

"Little mother," he wrote Mrs. Polk, "my chief difficulty is laughable in a sense, but from another point of view it is really a stupendous problem! One old mountaineer said to me last summer, 'Them schools is the courtin'est places in the world.' I begin to think he was right, and it is not always the superficial flirting and love-making which is a part of your coeducational schools,—a thing simply trivial and naughty,—but often tragic passion instead, quite in harmony with the title of Dryden's play, 'All for Love, or the World Well Lost'!

"Really, these children of the woods hear the call to mate as naturally as the birds in the trees, and knowing nothing of Fifth Avenue brown stone fronts or cozy cottages at Newport, they want to leave school, gather twigs and build their nests at once. And sometimes one feels as guilty in breaking up such prospective nests as when molesting a pair of birds!

"Am I getting to be something of a sentimentalist? Well, I assure you I am not going to let it grow upon me. I bear sternly in mind that, like the first pair of human beings in the Garden of Eden, they have really eaten of the tree of knowledge and know some things which they ought not to know,—having some secrets from the rest of mankind which are not at all good for them,—while the things they need to know for higher, better living are so numerous, that I ruthlessly break the tenderest hearts, and insist on study and discipline; for nothing but education, mental, moral and spiritual, will ever bring the greatest people in the world, the people of the Kentucky mountains, into their just inheritance! You see how completely identified I am again when I indulge in Kentucky brag,—which is not so different after all from the brag of other sections, and I promise not to let this grow upon me either, for work and not brag is before me, as you know. I want you to see, however, that I continue to feel the mountaineer is worth working for.

"But to return to the love-making. Tragedy and comedy are in evidence enough to lure me into the field of romance, but the practical hindrances to daily school work are too absorbing for great indulgence of my pen. Ardent swains pay open court to their sweethearts, promenading halls and grounds together and even pressing suit in the class room! While frequently the crowning difficulty in the whole matter is the pleased approval of parents! Early marriage, you know, is most common in the mountains, girls of twelve and thirteen often taking up the duties of wives and the great desire of parents for their daughters is usually to get them early married off.

"But,—I suspect this is all familiar to you," he reminded himself, "and still I must tell it to you,—and let you laugh over a recent experience I have had with a pair of lovers.

"You may be sure that I have lectured most earnestly and scientifically upon the evils of tobacco and liquor for the young, and also have set forth as tactfully and convincingly as I know how the fact that a school is not the place for lover-like attentions, beseeching them to give themselves wholly to the business of acquiring knowledge while they are here, with all the eloquence of which I am capable. But, in spite of this, as I was leaving my recitation room at the close of school a few days ago I noticed a girl, Alice Tomby, lingering with Joe Mott, one of her admirers, and stepping outside I found another admirer of hers standing beneath a near-by tree, with clenched fist and blazing eyes.

"I knew that a typical mountain tragedy was quite possible and stopping casually a moment to look at my watch, I turned and went back to find the girl and her beau in a most lover-like attitude.

"I threw my shoulders out to their broadest, and walked with all the dignity I could summon to my desk where I stood before them a moment in silence. Their sheepish faces were a study for the cartoonist, and I wanted to laugh more than I can tell you, but I finally said gravely:

"'Miss Tomby and Mr. Mott' (the use of the last name with Mr. or Miss, which is unusual in the mountains, is always most impressive), 'you are guilty of breaking a rule of the school. You must remain and write twenty times each the sentence I shall put upon the board.'

"Then an old song came suddenly into my mind and I wrote without quiver of lash or hint of smile the silly lines:

"'Frog went courting, he did ride,
Sword and pistol by his side.'

"'That!' said the fellow, looking startled, while the girl hung her head.

"'Yes, that,' I replied in perfect seriousness. And the two wrote the lines under my most calm, most dignified eye till they were thoroughly disgusted with themselves and one another. When at last they went out, the girl tossed her head and ignored both her crestfallen and her jealous lover. With books under her arm she went alone straightway to the boarding hall.

"The story of the discomfited lovers is spreading in the school, and the quotation of 'Frog went courting, he did ride,' hilariously given is quenching the ardour of many an amorous swain. Possibly a little wholesome humour may after all be more helpful than stern enforcement of rules, and you know if there is one thing more than another we mountain folks lack, it is a sense of humour! So, even on general principles, it will do no harm to cultivate it.

"However, with all this cruel separation of tender hearts perhaps I am in a fair way to become a cynical old bachelor instead of a sentimentalist."

He was determined to write cheerfully, for he knew that she constantly grieved over the alienation between Mr. Polk and himself, so his letters usually held bright accounts of his work, though sometimes he let her have a glimpse of the struggle which went on in his heart.

He wrote once after a contest with himself over natural desire for more congenial surroundings:

"Little mother, when things seem too sordid and commonplace and barren for endurance, as I confess they have a way of doing at times, I do crave a look into your dear face. But as I am too far away to see you clearly, I remember how you came down here and worked with dauntless courage and good cheer, and I take heart again. Then several things recently have contributed to make me ashamed of faint-heartedness, and I really think I am going to develop some stronger fibre.

"The pathos of the mountain desire for 'larnin" has come to me overwhelmingly lately. A woman came on foot forty miles over the mountains last week bringing her daughter and seven others of neighbours and friends to the school only to find there was no room for them. But so great was the mother's distress and so appealing her sacrifice and hardship in making the trip that one of our lady teachers took the daughter into her own room rather than see the mother disappointed. A few days later two boys came in having driven a pair of lean goats over thirty miles hitched to a rude cart, which held all the earthly possessions they could muster, the old father and mother walking behind,—all hoping to buy entrance to the school for the boys. They, too, were disappointed, for we are full to overflowing this year. Then to cap the argument for stout-heartedness on my part, I went for a stroll yesterday afternoon and came across a boy who is making one of the bravest fights for an education that I ever saw. I found him putting his shoulder to great boulders on the mountainside, rolling them down and then setting himself to break them in pieces for use in paving our little town,—for you must know that under the influence of the school it is beginning to strive for general improvement. The boy, whose father is a worthless fellow, works at rock-breaking till he earns enough to go to school a while; then, when the money is gone, he returns to work again with a pathetic patience which has stirred me deeply.

"So, mother mine, when I long for a sight of your face,—and an old-time hand-clasp from Mr. Polk, as I assure you I too often do, or when I crave the feast of books and the quiet student atmosphere of a city library, I am simply going to think on these things in the future."

The second summer in the mountains came on and was a repetition of the first. The school was getting more pupils than could be accommodated, it was true, but Steve felt that contact with the thought of education would help to further the general cause. Then, journeying about through the wilderness was also a means of gathering fresh material for his nature and hunting stories for boys.

There was a distinct drawing towards the Follets in his subconscious mind, the real objective of which he would scarcely admit to himself. He put from him suggestive pictures of curls and pinafores which memory and flitting dreams still flashed before him at times. He meant to go there some day for he wanted to express his gratitude for all the kindness of the past, but the time had not yet come. He must not for the present be diverted in the least from the purpose which was occupying him. He must repay Mr. Polk,—that was the thought which dominated him, and to that end he was frugally gathering all the money he could. As he had carried the fox skin through the wilderness when a boy, so now he carried the thought of that debt in his mind, and no robber in the form of pleasant indulgence should prevent him from meeting his obligation.

The second session passed, and he had learned how to handle his difficulties with better success, while his method of teaching was more definitely marked out and he found more leisure for the use of his pen. Fresh, bright stories with the breath of the mountains in them began to find ready sale, and occasionally as his pen dipped a bit into romance it brought more than ordinary returns. Upon the tide of this success came a strong temptation: Why not go to a distinctly literary atmosphere and make a business of literature? He felt an inward assurance of making good and a longing for the work which was almost overpowering. Money for the debt must continue to accumulate very slowly when so much time must be given to the daily business of teaching, for which he was very poorly paid, and he could not know freedom until that debt was paid. In literary work, too, he could combine the cause of mountain need with his daily task with equal effectiveness in both directions, for could he not portray with great pathos the mental, spiritual and material poverty of his people? And he stifled for the moment something within him which cried, "Others might do that, but never one of our own!" Beside all this it was probable, as Mr. Polk had said, that money was more sorely needed for schools than personal service and he believed by giving himself to literary work he could earn it. He had never been perfectly sure that giving his life to teaching and personal work among his people was the best method of helping them, so he need not feel chagrined by any inconsistency.

So great was the temptation which came to him at this crisis that he determined when the session closed to go for a visit to Mirandy's family and from there to the Follets, with the thought that he would not like to leave the mountains without seeing them, and it would doubtless be best to go east for his literary career. In this satisfactory justification of the latter visit he allowed himself the freedom of pleasant reminiscence about the spot where life first began to really unfold for him.

"Little Nancy," he said to himself, "why she must be nineteen now, clothed in long frocks and maidenly dignity, I suspect,—but I certainly hope she still wears the little white pinafores." And his eyes grew misty with a tenderness which he would have classified as brotherly, had it occurred to him to question himself. Then he smiled suddenly and said, "Yes, I must go and see about those pinafores before I leave the mountains."

He made the visit to Hollow Hut first, and in the ease of a saddle seat he reached the old familiar wood by a much more direct trail than he had followed when a boy. He halted his pony at last by the great boulder where Tige lay buried. The tragedy of his grief on that long-ago morning when he had touched the stiffened body of his old friend came back to him with such vividness that, in spite of "Time's long caressing hand," he could not "smile beholding it." He hitched his horse close by with a sense of the old dog's nearness and protection, for he meant to camp on that spot during his stay as he used to do when a boy. Then he went on foot down the mountainside to his old home in the hollow, little dreaming, as he passed along its rocky fastness, that a "still" was hidden there.

It was just dusk of an early June day, and cool shadows dropped their soft curtains about the old log house as he walked towards the door unannounced. He stopped a moment at the grave of his father and mother, and then followed noiselessly the little worn path to the cabin. As he drew near, he saw the fitful light of blazing pine-knots on the hearth and caught the sound of boisterous laughter. Reaching the door he stood a moment in the shadow of the outer darkness, before stepping into the light. Then,—what he saw transfixed him! White to the lips he watched a moment.

A group of men, Mirandy's husband among them, surrounded a little fellow about six years old, who, having been made reeling drunk, was trying to walk a crack in the floor. The little victim swayed and tottered and struggled under the hilarious urging of his spectators.

"Hit's Champ fer his pappy"

Steve's first mad impulse was to snatch up the wronged child, and, if necessary, face the half-drunken men in battle. But this would be worse than useless his second sober thought told him, for there stood Mirandy looking carelessly on from the kitchen door behind. The child was doubtless hers, and the father was taking part in the revolting deed! What could he do? He knew they would brook no interference.

With hard-won self-control he stepped upon the threshold, courteously lifted his hat and bade them "Good-evening."

Instantly the men turned and pistols clicked, for they thought him a revenue officer; but Mirandy, looking into his still boyish face which had caught the light, while his unfamiliar figure was in shadow, exclaimed:

"Don't shoot! Hit's Steve, my little buddie Steve!" And she stepped across the room to him in a way which showed she was capable of being stirred into action sometimes.

The men looked uncertain, but Mirandy's husband, peering into Steve's face a moment, said:

"Yes, that's right, hit's Steve Langly, though I'd nuver knowed ye in the world," and the other men dropped back.

The child in the centre of the room looked about with dull eyes, then dropped to the floor in a pitiful little drunken heap.

With his heart wrung to the point of agony, Steve stepped forward and stooping down lifted it tenderly to his breast. In the old home that little boy represented himself, as he used to be. When he could speak he said in a voice which trembled upon the silence:

"This is my little nephew, is it not?"

And Mirandy cried out sharply to her husband, without answering the question:

"Ye shan't nuver do that no more," and the men slunk out one by one, ashamed, rebuked, sobered, though they could not have told why.

Steve turned as they left and sat down, still holding the child to his breast. Then gently releasing his hold with one hand he tenderly pushed back the damp hair from the little swollen face, while Mirandy stood by, the tears dropping down her cheeks,—a thing most unusual for a mountain woman. And she said again passionately, "Champ shan't nuver make him drunk agin."

"What is his name?" asked Steve at last.

"Hit's Champ fer his pappy. The bigges' one—he's outdoors some'eres,— he's named Steve," she said in mollifying tone. "He was borned the nex' winter atter you was here, an' you'd been sech a likely lookin' boy I thought I'd name him fer ye."

"That was good ev you, Randy," said Steve dropping tenderly into the old form of speech. "I'll be glad ter see my namesake. Air the two all ye hev?"

"No, thar's the baby on the bed; she's a little gal," Mirandy replied dully. "Then there's two on 'em that died, when they was babies. We women allus gits chillun enough," she said, in a whining voice peculiar to the older women of the mountains which she had already acquired.

Steve remained a month and it was the most trying time of his life. When he learned of the "still," which he did very promptly, despair for Mirandy, her husband and the children filled his heart. Champ Brady was always under the influence of his "moonshine," and Steve knew it was perfectly useless to try to dissuade him from making or using it. Mirandy had his own distaste for it, but she had been accustomed to the thought of its free use all her life, and how could he make her listless mind comprehend its danger for her children? Not trusting her emotion and passionate protest the day he came, he talked with her earnestly many times and made her promise to do all she could to keep the children from it.

He took the two little boys, Steve and Champ, with their dog, every day up to the old haunt by Tige's rock, where he camped every night. He had brought picture books with him, illustrated alphabets and one-syllable stories with the thought of possible need for them. And the brown eyes of the two little fellows, so like his own in the old days, as he well knew, in their blankness and wonder, gave eager response to new things. He called the spot "our school," and the two little pupils soon learned their letters, while in a month's time little Steve was reading simple stories telling that "The dog is on the mat," and "The cat is on the rug" with great exhilaration, and spelling out laboriously more complex things.

But Champ Brady was restless under the visit. He told Mirandy frequently that he had no use for a fellow who hadn't enough stuff in him to drink good liquor when it was put before him; and Steve, knowing well his state of mind without hearing any expression of it, went sadly away from the cabin at Hollow Hut for the third time.

After a last earnest talk with Mirandy, he took the little boys to the old spot where they had kept school and he had camped for the month and put into the hands of Steve the second a German silver watch which he had also brought with the thought of a boy in the old home again as a possibility.

"This little shining ticker will tell you each day that you are going to make big, strong men who know things one of these days. You will listen to it always, will you not?" he said, and each in turn, as he was held up in the tender arms, promised earnestly with queer aching in their little throats. Then Steve set them down and rode away, looking back again and again with a waving hand at the two sober little figures as long as they were in sight.

"Oh, God of the wilderness," he cried, when at last he saw them no more, "Thou didst come and comfort me when I wandered here alone; oh, now give me assurance that Thou wilt watch over these two of my own blood and bring them into the light."

The prayer went up in despair akin to that of his boyhood's desolation and again, after a time, a sense of comfort and peace flooded his soul, while, in its full tide, a fresh resolve was fixed upon him:

"I will give my life to the work. Not money alone, please God, if I should make it, but my daily breath and life and vigour shall go for the uplift of my people of the mountains!"

And he smiled to think that literature should ever have appealed to him, for a sense of linking himself to the Almighty God to whom he had prayed had come to him in the holy stillness of the wilderness, making anything else seem trivial beyond compare.

He did not go to the Follets as he had intended, but made his way slowly back to the school, stopping at cabins here and there as in previous summers, chatting with the people, getting into their life and giving them visions as no alien could have done.

On this trip he passed a great coal mine and here he spent a couple of weeks watching the work with great interest. He carefully examined the various strata of the excavation and studied the practical working of the mine with keen intent, his college course having given him ample preparation for its intelligent comprehension.

Suddenly a bright thought struck him.

"Look here," he said to himself, "why not locate a mine here in the mountains, as Mr. Polk used to talk of my doing, buy the land for a few hundred dollars, as I am sure I can in some localities, and then make it over to Mr. Polk? He will know how to handle it, and if it is valuable will certainly make it pay. With another year's work I can have the money, and by that means I can cancel that debt with one fell stroke, perhaps," he went on jubilantly,—and if it proved to do so many times over, he would only be the more rejoiced, he thought.

XII

LOVE'S AWAKENING

Full of this happy inspiration Steve went back to his work, determined to gather during the year a sum sufficient to make his purchase, so as to be ready for the next vacation when he would be free to go prospecting. Under the stimulus of this good hope he worked with great absorption, only allowing himself the recreation of a weekly letter to Mrs. Polk, which he never failed to send, continuing to put into it all the interesting and amusing things which came into his work,—and they did come in spite of the seriousness of his life.

Oftentimes in brooding thought he went back to the little Steve who was duplicating his own early life in the old home. He had considered mountain educational work hitherto in the large; he began now to think of it from the nucleus of the home. How he would like to see the old spot of his boyhood redeemed by an ideal home life! And the thought touched many latent springs of his manly nature, calling forth dim, sweet visions of domestic love and beauty.

But he hushed nature's appeal peremptorily, he thrust back the visions with the firm decision that he had no leisure for dreams, and continued his many-sided work through another winter with accustomed constancy. It was in the early spring of that year when an unexpected telegram came to him from Mrs. Polk. It read:

"Meet Nita and myself at L—— to-morrow, 7 A. M. train".

How the brief message thrilled him! He had plodded so long alone. He sprang up from his place at the breakfast table where the message had been handed him, his eyes shining and his step buoyant. Securing leave of absence from school duties for a couple of days, he went at once to hire a team which would take him forty miles over the mountains to the railroad station.

Forty miles! With a good team and a buoyant spirit they seemed little more than so many city blocks. To look into the face and talk once more with the "little mother" would renew his enthusiasm for his work. She must have known that he was growing dull and spiritless with the lingering winter days,— —she had such a wonderful way of divining things. His eyes grew misty with tender recollection of her.

And Nita,—beautiful Nita Trowbridge,—when she should step out in the early morning light, it would be like flashing his glorious mountain sunrise upon some artist's masterpiece! And he was hungry for the beauty and grace and charm of the city which she embodied. Yes, it was true, there was no denying it! And fast and faster sped the retreating miles under his joyful expectations till the journey was ended, a night's refreshing sleep had passed and he stood at last at the little station, restlessly pacing up and down the platform, with eye and ear strained to detect the first hint of the incoming train.

Next he was rushing into the rear sleeper!

"Little mother!"

"Steve!" were the greetings as he took Mrs. Polk in his arms while the eyes of both brimmed with tears. Then turning quickly to Nita, he greeted her with less demonstration but with equal warmth.

Catching up their hand-bags he hurried them out, for through trains show scant respect for mountain stations, and leading the way to his waiting vehicle he helped Mrs. Polk in with easy confidence, then turned to Nita. What was it about her that made him instantly conscious that the spring wagonette was very plain, the newness long gone and that the horses, with abundant manes and tails, lacked trimness and style? He started to apologize for his turnout, then quickly set his lips. If he must begin apologizing here, where would it end?

"This is just a mild forerunner of the heights before you," he said laughingly, as he carefully helped her mount the high step before which she had stood uncertainly.

But the trip proved equally delightful for them all. The mountain air was bracing, the morning panorama spread out before them, gloriously beautiful as it always was, brought constant delighted exclamation from both Mrs. Polk and Nita while Steve found fresh enjoyment in their pleasure.

The little cabins which came into view on the way, standing bare and barren by the roadside, or looking out from forest recesses where there was hardly a road to follow, or clinging to some lofty "bench" upon the mountainside, all were fronted by poorly clad children gazing in solemn, open-mouthed interest while the strangers passed.

"Dear little things," said Mrs. Polk, "they stand in mute appeal to us to open a path for them out into our world,—to take them into the fold of our larger brotherhood."

Steve looked back into her bright, earnest face with kindling eyes, while Nita turned from one to the other with the old childish wonder again in her face. These mountain folk were a new species to her, interesting and amusing perhaps, but from whom she instinctively shrank. Not that she was in the least disdainful, she was of too sweet a nature for that, but she had no conception of a divine bond of human kinship which could ever include her and them.

They spent the night at a mountain village, breaking the long drive for the ladies, and the next day reached the school where Steve daily gave his best, and which was so dear to Mrs. Polk. During the two days following, as during the trip, Steve made them as comfortable as possible, still making no apologies for anything, and indeed no apology was necessary, for Mrs. Polk had known what to expect, and the royal hospitality which glorified it, while Nita accepted the one with simple good taste and the other with real, if not genial, appreciation. The visit was full of interest for Mrs. Polk as she noted the growth of the work, and Nita went about through school buildings and grounds, her beauty and tasteful attire making her a most observed visitor. Nor did she fail to show interest in the work, thoroughly courteous and kindly, and yet which somehow seemed detached.

As Steve followed her with admiring eyes and sincere regard, he could not help seeing most clearly that she could never fit into the mountain landscape. He thought whimsically of Mr. Polk's dreams for her and himself and knew that though he could have remained in her world and found happiness, she could never have come into his. His early intuition had not been at fault; she would never touch the height, breadth and depth of universal womanhood with its vision and its sympathy.

Just before leaving, the two visitors spent a recitation period in Steve's class room, and so eager was he to reveal the best in his pupils that he did not dream he was also putting forth the teacher's best.

When the pupils had filed out and the three stood alone, Mrs. Polk made a gay little bow, and said with glistening eyes:

"Bravo, Sir Knight of the Mountains, you have certainly won your spurs,— though they be of civilian make!"

He smiled in return, brought back to a consciousness of himself, but turning from it instantly again, he inquired:

"And what do you think of my brother knights?"

"They are equally fine," said Mrs. Polk warmly.

"They are indeed," joined in Nita, "but how you have penetrated the hopeless exteriors of these people, as we saw them on our way here, found the germs of promise and developed them, will always remain an unfathomable mystery for me," she declared. "I confess I understand your skill less than I do that of the sculptor who makes the marble express beauty, thought and feeling,—and his work would be infinitely more to my taste. I think nothing more distasteful than contact with people can be,—and when it must be daily——" She shrugged her shoulders in conclusion expressively.

Steve smiled back at her for he knew she did not think of him as one of these people with whom she could not bear the thought of daily contact.

"Now confess, don't you get dreadfully tired of it all?" she persisted, looking with real appeal into his face as though she would draw him away from it if she could.

"Unspeakably, sometimes," he smiled back again, then looking beyond her over the mountains he added simply, "but I belong here."

And uncomprehending as she would ever be, she turned at last lightly away and walking to the outer door stepped out upon the campus, leaving her sister and Steve for a little talk alone, which she was sure they would like.

When she was gone, Mrs. Polk laid a hand upon Steve's arm and said softly: "Some day, Steve, everything will come right," looking expressively into his eyes, and he knew she meant between himself and Mr. Polk, a subject that had not been mentioned since she came. "I catch beautiful prophecies sometimes of all this human desert blossoming as a rose," she went on with her old gay enthusiasm, "and I am fully persuaded now, as I never have quite been since you left us, that you have chosen your work wisely. I had to come at last and see for myself.

"But are you going to live your life alone, Steve, dear," she asked after a moment wistfully, "with no sweet home ties?"

"I do not know, little mother," he said gravely. His mind went instantly to the old cabin home and little Steve, but he couldn't tell even her of the family life there now,—nor yet of the mystic vision which had intruded upon his brooding thought.

His sudden smile flashed over the seriousness of his face as he replied at last, "I have been too busy and too poor to think about it so far."

She did not smile in return, but catching both his hands in hers she looked up at him with motherly insistence, and asked:

"Have you never loved any dear girl? Is there no sweet face that sometimes steals into the little home which nestles always in every true man's innermost heart?"

Her strong mother-love had surely lent her a mystic's insight and compelling power!

Instantly into the dim outline of the vision of his brooding thought which he had hitherto constantly thrust aside, came with a distinctness that startled him, a childish face framed in yellow curls above a little white pinafore!

He caught his breath with the vividness of it, then pulled himself together and looking down into the dear eyes of the woman who had been more than second mother to him, and who thereby had won the right to question him, he said with a curiously puzzled look:

"Why, I do not know,—perhaps so,"—then, as she still looked intently at him, "you have startled me. I have become such a stupid grind, I guess I need waking up. I will commune with myself, as I have never done before, and let you know what I discover," he ended more lightly.

She knew that a revelation had come to him in that moment and was content without further questioning. With a last gentle, loving pressure for his hands she released them and they walked out together to join Nita.

Their team was soon ready and after another long, pleasant drive Steve was watching the departing train from the little station platform. He felt keen regret as it bore his friends out of sight, but he turned to his team for the homeward drive with a strange exhilaration in his heart. He had hardly been able to wait for that communion with himself, and when the opportunity came there was no uncertainty in its tenor.

"Of course I love Nancy Follet! I have loved her ever since I first set eyes upon her sweet little face,—and it has come before me always in any stress of mind or heart as though to tell me she was always to have part in my life. And yet I have been so dull I did not understand. She preëmpted my heart from the first and that is why I did not love beautiful Nita Trowbridge,— why I have never been able to look at any girl with a spark of interest since." How he loved to linger over the revelation which had come to him! It was like having emerged from a desert into a land flowing with milk and honey. Little Nancy! She had been so gentle, so confiding, so eager to help him with things,—she would be his dear helper in the work of his life,—and the work would thereby be glorified beyond measure! Under the spell of his tender musing the forty miles again sped by unheeded and he was back once more at the schoolroom door.

It was well that his tasks for the year were well-nigh over, for he at once became consumed with the desire to see Nancy in the maturity of her girlhood. He promptly decided that he would go as soon as school closed and win her promise before he went on that prospecting tour. In the meantime his mind continued to hover over the hours they had spent together as boy and girl. He went to mill once more walking beside a little fairy figure on old Dobbin's back,—he caught the fragrance of shy flowers

- 78 -

which nestled in cool woodland depths, and memory let softly down the bars into a holy of holies as the little girl said again in her sweet innocence, "Steve, let's build us a house in this wood and live here always." He mounted the rugged steeps of Greely's Ridge, her strong protector, while she reached down once more a timid little hand to hold his tightly,—and suddenly he was startled with remembrance of the character of that ridge. It must have held minerals! Coal, yes, coal,—he was sure of it! There was the piece of land he had been wanting to find!

And so with buoyant, twofold hope he started as soon as school was out towards the Follet home, having deposited in the bank a sum which he felt would be sufficient to purchase the Greely Ridge, should he find it as valuable as he suspected and no one had preceded him in its discovery.

XIII

OLD TIES RENEWED

It was mid-afternoon of a late June day when Steve stopped at Mr. Follet's store. He wondered if his old friend would be there. Yes, the door was open, and for a moment Steve stood on the platform in front, his tall figure erect, his head bared as he looked reverently towards the little home which had opened the world of books to him. Then Mr. Follet's high voice rang out from the dark depths where dry-goods and groceries rioted in hopeless confusion as of old.

"Hello, stranger, what's the time o' day?"

Steve stepping forward put out an eager hand, and cried:

"Mr. Follet, don't you know me?"

But the man only stared, coming forward into the light of the doorway.

"Never saw you before," he declared at last; "or if I did, can't tell where under the cano*pee* 'twas."

Steve laughed with keen enjoyment at hearing the familiar old expression, and said eagerly:

"Don't you remember Steve, little Steve Langly who worked for you one summer?"

"Steve!" exclaimed Mr. Follet; "of course I do; nobody at my house has forgotten him, not by a jugful,—but this ain't Steve!"

"This *is* Steve though, Mr. Follet,—the same Steve, with just as grateful a heart for you and Mrs. Follet as I had the day I left you about a dozen years ago."

"Well, this does beat me," said Mr. Follet. "We'll lock right up and go over to the house. My wife and Nancy will be powerful glad to see you if they can ever think who under the cano*pee* you are." And he stepped briskly about locking up, and then the two walked over to the house.

Mrs. Follet was seated on the piazza with some light sewing when they came up, and to Mr. Follet's excited introduction of Mr. Langly she made polite but unrecognizing acknowledgment, and her husband was too impatient to delay his revelation.

"Why, ma, you don't tell me you don't know Steve," he exclaimed.

"Steve," returned Mrs. Follet bewildered.

- 80 -

"Why, yes! little, old, scrawny, mountain Steve," exclaimed Mr. Follet, "who did everything that was done here one summer!"

Then Mrs. Follet slowly grasped the astonishing thought that little ignorant Steve and the fine-looking young man before her were one and the same, and gave him gentle, motherly greeting.

"Where's Nancy?" went on Mr. Follet, impatiently.

"She's gone with Gyp for a gallop," returned Mrs. Follet, "but she ought to be back any minute now." And by the time they had exchanged brief accounts of the years that had passed since they last met, Nancy was seen swaying gracefully down the road upon her pony's rounded back. She waved gaily as she passed the porch not noticing the stranger who was somewhat screened by hanging vines, and then she turned into the lane which led to the stable.

Steve's eyes glistened at the vision of the girl which time had so charmingly matured, and starting up he exclaimed:

"Let me meet her at the stable where I used to help her on and off old Dobbin's back," and with a bound he was off the porch and striding towards the lane.

Nancy had slowed her pace along the shady driveway, and Steve, going noiselessly through the grass, was at her side when she was ready to dismount.

Smilingly he held out his hand for her to step upon, his glowing eyes lifted to hers. Startled she drew back, her eyes held and fascinated, however, by his intent gaze.

For a long instant they gazed, and then she breathed:

"Oh, Steve!"

Had the meeting occurred otherwise, she probably would never have taken the tall, broad-shouldered, handsome young fellow for the Steve of her childish memory, but she only saw and recognized those brown eyes lifted to hers as they used to be in the old days when he took her from Dobbin's back, with the same tender light in them.

"Yes, Nancy, it's Steve!" he exclaimed joyfully. "And you knew me after all these years!"

A smile that held something sweet and sensitive flashed assent, and then in reaction from the stir of undefined feeling, which she was not ready to acknowledge, her eyes danced with sudden humour. Keeping her saddle she glanced behind her to the pony's back, and said:

"Where are our bags of meal?"

Steve laughed in responsive gaiety, and in spite of himself let his eyes rest upon her in kindling admiration.

"Oh, I see good grist which the mill of time has ground for you," he said, and put out his palm again for her to step upon.

But she, flushing with girlish surprise at his ready gallantry, which showed how completely the little mountain boy had been lost in the cultured man, drew back once more and with equal quick wit said, laughing:

"You will certainly find it has, and in good, substantial material if you try to take my weight in your hand."

"The same mill has ground out for me an adequate amount of muscle," he declared, adding with a hint of pleading in his voice, "You must let me renew old times," and without further protest she lightly touched his hand with her foot as she sprang from the pony's back.

"Weight doesn't count with so light a touch as that," laughed Steve, and started to lead the pony into the stable, when a coloured boy stepped up to care for it.

"You see we keep a groom these days," said Nancy.

"Yes; what style the mountains are taking on," returned Steve, as Nancy gathered up the long skirt of her riding habit, and the two walked together through the grass to the porch.

"To what an astonishing height you have grown," said she with naive charm, looking up at him.

"You have done equally well," he returned, measuring with his eye her slender length; then he added with his sudden smile which held the whimsical quality of old friendship, "Please tell me,—where are the curls?"

"Oh, they are tucked snugly away out of sight," said she demurely, with a pretty gesture which straying tendrils had made habitual, and the warm colour rising again to her face.

"There should be a law against carrying curls concealed," said he.

By this time they were at the porch, and as they resumed the family exchange of items of interest from each side, Steve and Nancy sitting on the steps as in the old days, he saw the fair dream-structure of the past few weeks in the beginning of complete realization.

In the evening as Mr. and Mrs. Follet, Steve and Nancy sat again on the porch enjoying the night air after a warm day, they talked interestedly of old times and the changes which had taken place. Steve found that Crosscut, the little flag station over which Mr. Follet presided, had expanded into a small straggling town with a meeting-house, school of uncertain sessions and a thriving saloon.

As they chatted pleasantly a young man turned into the gate and came up the path with a debonair swing that proclaimed him much at home.

"Howdy everybody," he said jauntily, and Nancy rose with pleasant greeting for him. Then turning to Steve she introduced Mr. Colton to Mr. Langly.

Steve met the newcomer with quiet courtesy, while Mr. Colton responded with cordiality of the "hail-fellow-well-met" type, and immediately seated himself beside Nancy with an air of proprietorship.

Very soon Mr. Follet in the course of conversation turned and addressed Steve by his first name.

"Steve!" exclaimed the visitor. "Didn't Miss Nancy introduce you to me as Mr. Langly? Are you Steve Langly who visited Louisville with a Mr. Polk some ten or twelve years ago?"

"I am," said Steve with much surprise.

"Is that so?" returned Mr. Colton with enthusiasm. "Well, I am Raymond Colton!"

"Indeed," exclaimed Steve heartily. "Well, this is pleasant."

"I should say so," returned Raymond. "I tell you, old fellow, we never forgot that lickin' you gave us at our school—served us right and did us good." He launched into a hilarious account of that experience which everybody enjoyed, and there was a little pleasant, general conversation. Then Raymond suddenly exclaimed:

"Miss Nancy, where's your banjo?" and went at once for it.

"I tell you, Steve, she can play on the old banjo and sing as no one else ever did," he said as he returned and laid it in her lap.

Nancy turned to Steve with a quick flush which showed even in the moonlight and protested: "I really don't know a thing about it, only what father taught me when I was a little girl."

And Mr. Follet said excitedly, "You see, Steve, she was so lonesome after you left I had to get the old thing down to cheer her up. I hadn't played any on it since I was a young fellow courtin' her mother. I don't believe I'd ever got her without that banjo," he added and laughed with great good humour. "Nancy don't think much of it," he went on. "She thinks it's nothin' beside the piano, but Raymond, here, is like me, he thinks it beats the piano all hollow."

"Sing 'Robin Adair,'" put in Raymond, and Nancy began striking soft minor chords for a little prelude. Then a rich, contralto voice, low and clear, told the tender old story of Robin Adair and his love, which the banjo echoed with little improvised hints of the air. Raymond and Mr. Follet called for one song after another of the old favourites, Raymond often joining in with a fine tenor, which harmonized perfectly with Nancy's contralto. At last she sang of her own accord "The Rosary."

There was an exquisite pathos in the beautiful, heart-breaking notes that stirred Steve deeply. What depth of feeling, as well as maidenly reserve and charm, his little Nancy had developed! The curls and pinafores were gone, it was true, but as he watched her sweet, expressive face in the moonlight and felt the fullness of her sympathy and understanding in the singing, he said to himself, "I am willing to lose them for this!"

"Miss Nancy, please don't ever sing that any more; it gives me the shivers," said Raymond and was seconded by Mr. Follet.

"It's bedtime for old folks, anyhow," the latter went on, and added, "I guess Steve's tired enough to go, too," and though Steve was not ready to admit this, Raymond gave him gay good-night and he followed his host to the little attic room where he had slept as a boy, and which Mrs. Follet had made ready for him, because he had insisted that it was just the place for him. The house was small and he knew somebody must vacate comfortable quarters if he slept elsewhere.

But once in the old bed Steve did not find fair memories crowding about as he had anticipated. Even the echoing sweet songs lost their melody. Indeed he could think of nothing but the fact that Nancy and Raymond Colton sat together on the front porch, left there by her parents as though he had special rights. A midnight thunder-storm caught up his perturbed thought with noisy energy.

"But why not!" he exclaimed sadly for the hundredth time to his rebellious heart. "You certainly have no claim."

But that lately aroused, throbbing fountain of love's pulsations replied with vehemence: "I have! I have loved her every moment since I first looked upon her as a little girl, and I love her in her sweet maturity with all my soul. She is mine!"

So the wordy war went on between his good sense and his yearning heart, banishing every dear, cherished memory and postponing sleep till the wee morning hours.

Next day after the breakfast dishes were done, Mrs. Follet proposed that Nancy take Steve for a ride with Gyp and the family horse over to the Greely woods, their old favourite haunt, and this exactly suited Steve, for, in spite of the night's disturbance, nothing could please him more than an opportunity for companionship with Nancy alone, and he was still impatient to see if his memory of that rugged ridge of woodland was correct.

He went out at once to saddle the horses. It was a crisp, cool, clear morning after the storm, and Nancy soon appeared in a trim riding habit and cap with deep visor to shade the eyes. The severe lines and dark blue of her costume made charming contrast to her softly rounded face, with its delicate colouring and the stray yellow tendrils of hair which were always slipping out from the fluffy braids which bound her head. She surely was fair to look upon, and when Steve had assisted her to mount in the old way,—holding out his hand and she stepping upon it in laughing ease,—she sat her pony with the graceful poise of the true Kentucky girl, making a picture which less partial observers than Steve could not have failed to find full of charm. They cantered off briskly down the road.

When they reached the wood Steve grew keenly reminiscent, as had become his habit the last few weeks. Forgetting Raymond completely, the past came back to him vividly; he seemed to feel again Nancy's confiding trust in him,—and he yearned to know how clearly she remembered. He looked often upon her as she rode beside him, the two horses touching noses in the narrow path, but the delicate face revealed nothing.

"Do you remember," he said at last, "what a veritable slave you made of me in this old wood?"

She laughed brightly and replied, "Why no, I haven't any such recollection."

"Well, you knew even then just how to do it," he returned with a bit of insinuation. "You would look up at the tallest, hardest tree to climb and see some high-hanging blossom which you coveted, and I immediately scaled the tree's height to lay the blossom at your feet."

She laughed again and her cheeks this time flushed a rosy hue, unaccountably disconcerting to her.

"But that, after all, was as it should have been," he went on after a moment, smiling. "We men need your bidding to send us to the heights, always."

"I do not agree with you," she said, recovering her poise instantly; and summoning a girlish perversity, she led him straightway from sentiment to the substantial. "Each one must mount up in his own strength, like these splendid old trees, without prop or help, only the light from above to draw it upward," and a very demure look crossed her ever-changing face as she finished the little speech.

"You are right," said Steve smiling and remembering Mrs. Polk's lesson from the giant beech so long ago. "And yet, after all, many things help the tree in its growth besides the light from above,—the sun. There are the winds and the rain, and"—he paused a moment,—"its mates. Don't you know a tree rarely stands alone unless man has cut down its companions. They like comradeship. I believe they are dependent upon it in ways we do not know."

"How stupid of me to forget I was talking with a professor," said Nancy archly.

"And worse still for me to forget that I was trying to enlighten the lady who initiated me into the world of books," replied he promptly, yielding to her mood.

"Oh, how lovely that graceful, clinging vine is," she exclaimed, ignoring his retort and pointing up to a vine covered tree, while Steve thrust back into the secret place of his heart all the cherished memories which the old wood held for him, realizing decidedly that Nancy was no longer a shy, timid little girl ready to place her hand in his, but a young woman who would need to be wooed before she was won,—even though there were no Raymond.

"What had he expected anyway?" he reiterated sternly. "That she would be waiting his coming, all ready for the plucking?" He straightened himself in the saddle. He had long since learned how to work and wait for things he wanted; he could do it again.

He led the conversation away from the personal. They talked of nature, each finding under the spur of companionship many new interests in the old wood; and being a devoted nature lover, Steve was pleased to find that Nancy had added to her tender interest in the feathered folk much information as to peculiar characteristics of varying species. It was an easy transition from nature to nature's interpreters, the poets, and the two found mutual interest in recalling some choice things of literature. She had spent four years at a fine old Kentucky college, graduating in June with high honours. There was still a sweet seriousness about her as in the little Nancy of old, in spite of her girlish gaiety, and while the years of study had brought her an unmistakable breadth and culture, there was also a quaint freshness of speech and manner that made her especially attractive. Steve found keen satisfaction in the conversation, for the girl understood his view-point and yet had fresh conceptions of her own which she knew how to express.

He said to himself as he studied her (which having put aside the personal he could now do), "She has the New England alertness of mind inherited from her mother without the New England reticence, and from her Kentucky father, eccentric as he is, she gets the vivacity and charm which is the Kentucky girl's birthright."

And yet in the midst of his enjoyment an insistent despair of heart returned as he recalled a certain good fellowship in her attitude towards Raymond, which was missing with him. Obtuse as lovers usually are, it never occurred to him that this was one of the best of symptoms in his favour!

They had gone in leisurely fashion through the wood, but the tall trees began to drop away at last, and they went down the slope till the old mill stood before them in soft, quaker-gray upon the bank of a turbulent, rushing mountain creek. The big, wooden wheel had fallen from its place and the old mill itself was fast dropping into complete decay, but the trees in fresh summer green still hung affectionately over it. Just beyond the mill nestled the gray log cabin with its porch across the front; and, yes, there was Tildy pacing back and forth at her spinning-wheel just as she used to do when Steve and Nancy were children. She was of the thrifty type of mountain women, always cleanly, always busy, making the most of the meagre means at hand. To the young people it was as though some magic lantern had flashed before them a scene from the past, and the two turned involuntarily to one another with a rush of something tender upon their faces.

Without speaking they rode to the door, and before Steve could dismount Nancy had sprung from the saddle, caught up her skirt, and was warmly shaking hands with the old woman, whom now she did not often see. Steve quickly followed, and with the air of an old friend also, put out his hand cordially to Tildy.

She took it doubtfully, saying:

"Howdye, stranger?"

"Tilda pacing back and forth at her spinning-wheel"

"Why, don't you know me, Mother Greely?" Steve asked.

"I shore don't," she replied, pushing her spectacles up on her nose and peering earnestly through them. "No," she said finally, "I nuver seed ye afore; leastways I ain't no recollection of hit ef I ever did."

The old man, who with the old mill had fallen into decrepitude, then came slowly hobbling out, an inquiring look on his kind old face. Tildy turned to him, raising her voice shrilly, for he heard with difficulty and asked: "Nat, have ye ever seed this young man afore?"

"No," the old man returned after searching scrutiny.

Then Steve said: "Don't you remember an old gray horse that used to come to the mill with a little girl in white pinafore on his back, two bags of corn behind her, and a tousled, brown-haired boy of about twelve walking beside her?"

"And the little girl was always on the verge of starvation, and only molasses cakes could rescue her," put in Nancy laughing.

"Nancy and Steve," exclaimed the old woman, and then with the intuition of her sex for romance, she further exclaimed: "An' ye hev done got married!"

"No," Steve hastened to say; but the old man, more accustomed to his wife's shrill voice, caught her affirmation, and failed to hear Steve's denial.

"Well, now," said he, rubbing his hands together, greatly pleased, "Tildy and me allus said ye'd marry some day; ye was jes' suited to one another."

Nancy hated herself for flushing so unreasonably again, and Steve, not daring to look towards her, was hurrying to the rescue, when the old woman with a swift, keen glance at both, broke in with:

"No, pap, no they hain't," piped shrilly into the old man's ear.

His face dropped with evident disappointment, and there was an embarrassed moment for all of them.

"Mother Greely," said Nancy gaily, determinedly recovering herself, "have you got any of those molasses cakes you used to give us when we came over?"

"Wal now, I think I hev," said the old woman, rising as quickly as her stiffened limbs would let her.

Steve looked down at Nancy as Tildy went in, smiled, and said:

"Shall we sit on the door-step, as we used to?"

Nancy's eyes did not meet his, and she turned her head to hide that provokingly rising colour as she sat down in a matter-of-fact way.

When they rode away from the mill, having made the aged couple happy with the renewal of old times, Steve again with eager yearning strained his inner vision for a glimpse into her heart, but she betrayed not the slightest consciousness of the embarrassing episode.

As the horses went leisurely back along through the wood, Steve and Nancy talked gently of the two old people with their wondrous mountain combination of barest poverty, dense ignorance, keen intelligence, simple kindliness and gentle dignity,—qualities which the young folks were now prepared to recognize.

"It is curious how like two people grow from constant association," said Steve at last, musingly. "The resemblance between the old miller and his wife is striking, isn't it?"

"Yes, it is," returned Nancy; "the shape of face and type of feature is the same in both, and as for expression, each might be a mirror for the other."

"It would be interesting to know which had most influenced the other," said Steve; "whether she has conformed to his type or he to hers."

"Old Nat and Tildy certainly furnish a good opportunity for study of that problem," said Nancy, "for there has been little except the influence of each upon the other to leave its impress."

"The subject is an interesting field for the aspiring investigator," Steve went on. "I wonder that some fine-spun, scientific theory has not already been advanced,—but it only remains another formidable matrimonial hazard," he ended with his sudden smile.

"It does indeed," laughed Nancy. "Wouldn't it be dreadful to think of growing daily more and more like some people?"

"And on the other hand," promptly returned Steve, "how delightful to think of growing more and more like certain other people," turning to her with a light in his eye.

"But then there is the uncertainty,—which is most likely to influence the other," said Nancy, switching dexterously away from hinted personal application, and then with a dash of daring gaiety, adding, "When you marry a girl with a crooked nose, will yours begin to crook likewise, or will hers take on your symmetrical lines?"

"But I am not going to take one with a crooked nose," said Steve, smiling significantly in spite of himself.

"Perhaps not, but the question remains,—which is most likely to conform, a husband or a wife," said Nancy, shying back to the abstract again, with pretty positiveness. And then she called gaily, as she touched Gyp with her whip and started both horses off on a brisk canter, leaving the wood for the road, "Please let me know if you solve the problem, so I may be relieved in mind or forewarned."

As she dashed on slightly ahead of him, spirit and beauty in every line of pony and rider, Steve said to himself with a quizzical smile:

"How cleverly she manages to keep me at arm's length. Oh, little Nancy, where did you learn such tactics?" and he did not know that "such tactics" were sure forerunners of surrender.

As for Nancy, she stood a little later by her bedroom window. The trim, smart riding-habit was laid aside and a little light muslin of almost childlike simplicity had taken its place. She stood looking out at nothing through brimming tears, with flushed cheeks and quivering lips.

"I do blush so horridly when I am with him, and I'm afraid I say things I shouldn't. Oh, what makes me, when I do like him so much!"

XIV

"ALL RIGHT, SON"

After dinner Steve walked over to the store with Mr. Follet, talked with him a little, and then strolling up the street afterwards, he was joined with great cordiality by Raymond Colton.

The talk was breezy as was inevitable with Raymond. He had graduated at a great northern university in June, had any amount of *sang froid* and had as yet caught no glimpse of life save as a field for pleasure.

"What do you think of Miss Nancy?" he inquired enthusiastically. "Isn't she the prettiest thing going? I have seen them north, south, east, and west, but I honestly believe I never saw a sweeter flower growing than Nancy Follet!" he went on without waiting for Steve to answer his question, so a smile was all the response which seemed necessary.

"I came here," went on Raymond, "to look after a land proposition for father. They say there's lots of valuable coal and iron ore about here. I've dipped a good deal into that sort of thing at college and father sent me up to make some tests for him, and if I found anything rich to take up a 'claim' instanter. I've been here three weeks and I haven't done a thing yet. Miss Nancy has fascinated me so, I haven't had eyes for sordid things. But there's plenty of time; no danger of anybody's rushing in ahead in this sleepy little burg."

"I'm not so sure of that," returned Steve quietly. "You never know when somebody may slip in ahead of you. Business competition is a very lively thing I've been told, though I confess I don't know much about it," he ended easily.

"Well, I've been getting a good bit of experience in business here and there, and I can tell that there's nobody hanging about here that has much business go." He had no intention of being personal and Steve bowed, smiling remotely.

After some more desultory talk they separated and Steve went back to join Nancy on the porch where he thought he would find her.

Raymond looked after him with a half smile.

"Poor old Steve," he said to himself, "he's caught already, and the worst of it is, I am afraid he's got the best chance. She's a dear little chum with me, loves to sing to my tenor and laugh at my foolishness, but I noticed last night the blushes were for him." And his handsome face set into unusual, firm lines as he went on: "But I am going to win her! I'll do it in spite of him. To-night I'll walk off with her whether or no, and he'll think his case is lost, for he doesn't know girls, I can see that." And with restored confidence he went over to the store to visit Mr. Follet. He and Mr. Follet were on fine terms, and he spent an hour or so at the store every day. They seemed in fact to have some project in common requiring much consultation.

Evening brought Raymond again to the Follet porch, and after a little music and general talk, turning to Mrs. Follet he said:

"Mother Follet, won't you let us children, Miss Nancy and me, go for a little walk together? It is so hard for us to sit still." He said it with mock childishness that was irresistible, and without waiting for Mrs. Follet's consent, he laughingly grasped Nancy's hand and made off with her, whether or no.

Steve could not see the laughing but real protest in Nancy's face, and his lips set firmly as he watched her white frock swaying gently up the long, straggling street.

Mrs. Follet then went in and Mr. Follet, turning to Steve, began in pleased excitement:

"Raymond's mightily in love with her, ain't he?" and went on without waiting for a reply, "I can't tell about her,—you never can tell nothin' about girls, anyway, you know, and she's just wrapped up in her piano music. She spends hours thumpin' on what she calls classical music, but I wouldn't give it for one tune on the banjo. She's been begging me to let her go to New York and study, but Lord, she knows as much now as any woman under the cano*pee*'s got use for, I think, and I've told her she can't do it. Raymond says, though, she ought to go, and that he'd like nothin' better than to give her the chance. His folks have got money, I reckon, and he can do it all right. If anything'll help to get her that will."

Steve laughed in reply with as good grace as he could, and soon followed Mrs. Follet to bed as one of the "old folks" before the "children" returned.

It was evident enough that he did not count with anybody except the Greelys as a possible suitor for Nancy, and his sturdy heart chafed in almost bitter protest. Again sweet memories played truant in the small attic chamber. "And little Nancy has musical aspirations," he thought. "With the life I have chosen I could never gratify her. It is absolutely hopeless for me,—I have nothing to offer her. I am old and staid, anyway," he said finally to his rebellious heart. "I have known the responsibilities of life too long, and Nancy is made only for joy."

The next morning, putting aside his depression sternly, Steve went on horseback alone, taking the same road he and Nancy had taken the morning

- 92 -

before. He lingered again in the Greely woods, this time on a prospecting tour testing here and testing there carefully.

When he at last rode up to the little one-roomed log cabin the old folks again made him welcome. After chatting a goodly length of time with them, and getting his voice well pitched for the old man's hearing, Steve asked if Mr. Greely would not like to sell off some of his land.

The old man looked surprised at the question, for no coal fields had then been opened up in that part of Kentucky, so that he was not aware of the value of coal bearing land.

"Wal, course I would, but nobody would want ter buy hit. Thar's only this patch the cabin and mill sets on what's any a'count, an' that I want ter keep long's me an' the ole woman lives."

"I am sure you are mistaken about that, Mr. Greely. I think all that woodland ridge is good land, and I would like to own it. Will you and Mrs. Greely think it over, give me a price on it by to-morrow and let me have the first chance at it?"

Astonished beyond measure the old man looked helplessly at his wife.

"Why, Steve, give me what ye think hit is wuth, if you really want hit."

"Mr. Greely, I must tell you frankly that I cannot give what I think it is worth, but I can pay you more a thousand times than you can ever get out of it, for you are too old to attempt anything with it, and there are no children. I think it can be made to yield returns in ways of which you do not dream or I wouldn't buy it, but I do not *know* and I am making a venture in buying it."

The old man thought a minute, then said: "Wal, I know as much now about hit as I will ter-morror and you can have hit fer a hundred dollars, ef ye kin pay that much."

"No, Mr. Greely, I can't take it for that," said Steve smiling; "it will be worth much more to me if it is worth anything. I am willing to venture more on it," and he named a much larger sum than the one asked.

The old man could not speak for amazement. He had never heard of any one in "them parts" having so much money at one time and the trade was practically closed at once.

He left the old folks feeling like millionaires and felt immense satisfaction himself that the deal had progressed so well. If the old couple should live in luxury, as they might conceive the word, for the rest of their lives, they could never spend that sum in the mountains.

Steve knew the lay of the land for miles around and he felt sure there was nothing so valuable as the Greely Ridge with the railroad lying not far from its base.

Asking the Follets if he might leave his traps there for a few days he went at once in the afternoon to the county seat to take the necessary steps for the transfer of the land, and found the title perfectly clear.

With elation over the assured deal and happy expectation of more than cancelling his debt, he telegraphed Mr. Polk what he had done. A reply came promptly back saying, "I will be on at once and bring expert."

It was with mingled feelings that Steve thought of the meeting as he busied himself with the details completing the transaction, going over with a notary public for the old folks to sign the papers, getting everything ready for Mr. Polk's signature as purchaser since he was coming and one transfer would be sufficient. He did not stop at the Follets, but returned at once to meet his old friend.

When Mr. Polk stepped from the train and looked again upon the boy he had loved as his own, he put an arm about him, as he used to in the old days, and said:

"How are you, son?"

"Well, thank you," answered Steve, and both voices trembled a little.

That was all, but it restored the old frank relations. They talked with great interest about the purchase and went as soon as possible with the expert to get his opinion upon it. When careful tests of the property had been made, the expert was enthusiastic.

"I believe it will prove to be a rich coal deposit, and if well managed ought to bring you a small fortune."

That night when they returned to the little "hotel," so named, Mr. Polk and Steve talked long and interestedly over plans for developing the mine. Mr. Polk had pretty well-defined ideas for the immediate organization of a company and the beginning of operations.

Finally he turned to Steve and said:

"Son, I have grown since you left,—I hope, some wiser, and that little woman made me see before I left home that I had no right to dictate to you what you should do with your life. I know you have worked hard these three years, or you never could have saved money enough to buy this piece of land, even at so small a price, and I don't doubt you have done good at the same time.

But I still feel that you might do just as good work perhaps by earning money for the cause you are so greatly interested in, so I am going to make a proposition to you. Suppose you take the oversight of this mining business, handling the money and seeing that everything goes straight. We could well afford to pay you a good salary for this service and give you some shares in the company too. Then you can live right here and exert your influence upon your people, as you call them, at the same time."

Steve listened intently, and the thought of money, and Nancy and music lessons, while he remained in the mountains, made his brain whirl.

Finally he put out his hand. "You hev allus been kind an' generous ter me," he said uncertainly, with emotion which carried him back for an instant to the old-time speech. Then lifting his head he smiled and added, "Let me think of this till to-morrow."

Mr. Polk agreed, and they separated for the night.

It was again a time of sore temptation for Steve. All night he tossed and thought. In spite of recurring depression he had not given up hope of winning Nancy. Her desire for musical advantages had been the most discouraging thing of all, however, and if he accepted this offer, he could hope to give her what she wanted, while since Raymond was not accepted he felt free to win her if he could. He pictured the future with increasing exhilaration, as the night approached its zenith, the time of keenest mental activity; and then, as the ebb came with the waning hours, suddenly a little figure reeled and staggered as it tried to walk a crack in a cabin floor, and springing from bed Steve strode to the window, and looked out upon the silent, starry sky.

"Oh, God," he said, "keep me from temptation;" and after a time he went back to bed firm in the old resolution that whatever the sacrifice involved, he would give himself, and not money alone, to the work. And then he slept.

Next morning he smiled his sudden smile as Mr. Polk looked keenly into his face, and said:

"I guess I am incorrigible, Mr. Polk,—I can't see it except in the old way."

"All right, son," said Mr. Polk quietly, and when they separated it was with a warm hand-clasp as Mr. Polk exacted a promise that Steve would visit them his first opportunity. "'The little mother' longs to see her boy," he said affectionately; then added, "Some day we hope to be in shape to help you with your work."

When he was gone Steve left for the Follets again. A great peace had come upon him with the renewal of his resolution, and his heart leaped at the prospect of seeing Nancy again.

- 95 -

"How long it seems since I left her," he laughed to himself, and the thought sprang to his mind from out the ever active realm of human hope: "Perhaps I shall win her yet by some miracle!"

XV

FLICKERING HOPE

It was with keen satisfaction that Steve caught a glimpse of Nancy's white dress out under the trees upon his return to the Follets. He hurried over to the bench where she sat.

"Is there anything more satisfying than these Kentucky mountains?" he said, with enthusiasm, as he seated himself beside her. "There is something that constantly assures me I belong to them."

"I have wondered that you were not captured by the city with all its allurements," said Nancy.

"No," returned Steve, "though perhaps I might have been at first had not my little foster-mother been loyal to Kentucky mountain need. But my experience the past three years as teacher has made it impossible for me to ever get away from the outstretched hand of Kentucky mountain children," and his voice dropped into deep earnestness.

"I can understand how you feel," said Nancy after a little silence. "I could not help being interested in the school when it was opened here. Little children came trudging in from the most barren cabin homes, wide-eyed, and eager to 'larn,' and grown-up men and women tramped barefoot miles and miles every day to try to get some of the 'larnin' they'd heard about. Then they would plod away with the utmost patience trying to read and write. It was intensely pathetic. Nothing has ever touched and interested me so much as some supply work I have done for our school," she added, a light upon her face, which thrilled Steve's heart anew. What a help she could be to him in his chosen work!

"I am so glad you have felt the appeal of mountain need," said he, struggling to keep the thrill out of his voice. And then he told her of his hopes and plans, of the dream he had of a new school within reach of Hollow Hut, a region to which new possibilities were about to come, he had learned at the county seat, through a projected railroad line. Of how he hoped to have help in the work from Mr. and Mrs. Polk and perhaps other capitalists of the north, and she was most interested, most appreciative, showing all the sweet seriousness of little Nancy of old.

But this long talk of some two hours which revealed again congenial tastes and ideals of life for the two only served to make Steve's heart more intensely rebellious when, after supper, Raymond walked in once more with his debonair proprietorship of Nancy. As it happened she had just stepped out under the trees to get a bit of fancy work left there in the afternoon, and

- 97 -

Raymond joining her, barricaded the way to the house, insisting that the "old folks" were glad to get rid of them, till she laughingly sat with him there. It had been purely accidental, her going out just then, and she remained with inward protest, but Steve could only see in it complete surrender to the ardent suitor.

Mrs. Follet had not yet come out and Mr. Follet turned to Steve, laughing in a pleased way.

"I don't mind telling you, for I know you are interested," he said confidentially, "that Raymond told me this morning he was simply crazy about her, he couldn't wait any longer, and was going to pop the question to-night. I s'pose there ain't much question about it though, for I reckon she's as much in love as he, though,—as I said, you never can tell."

And he little suspected that what he said seemed to Steve the death-knell to his hopes.

Mr. Follet continued loquaciously: "Raymond's the greatest fellow I ever saw. Everybody likes him. Why, he's in with the moonshiners about here hand and glove, and they're powerful offish. Never saw anything under the cano*pee* like him. He has big plans too, about some of the land round here which he says is full of coal. He's looked a little at the Greely Ridge; he thinks that's the finest piece, but he hasn't been over it carefully yet—been too much in love, you know," and he laughed contentedly.

Steve made conventional reply, and admitting he was quite tired, went to the little attic for another restless, unhappy night.

If the good fairies had only visited his couch and whispered their story of what was going on under the trees, how sweet would have been his sleep! But they did not.

Next morning Steve announced at the breakfast table that he must be leaving the following morning; a few days off from work for pleasure was all he could take with good grace.

Mr. and Mrs. Follet expressed their regret, while Nancy's eyes were upon her plate. Mr. Follet was complaining of some sciatic pain, but tried to throw it off with his usual nervous energy.

"Nancy," he said, "you haven't taken Steve over to Borden's Cave, which has been discovered since he was here. Why don't you go this morning?"

"Why, I should be glad to," responded Nancy, and Steve, feeling that her agreement was upon the basis of the old family relationship between them, made no excuse, though he did not doubt, with the fatality of anxious lovers, that the engagement had taken place. The two started off with Gyp and the family horse for a three mile canter, and Steve's spirit rose with the exhilaration of it in spite of himself.

The cave proved to be a most interesting rock formation and when they had examined it, Steve pointing out some curious scientific facts, they sat down in the quiet woods upon a fallen tree trunk, while the horses grazed.

Nancy looked up at him when they were seated, and said naively:

"How much you have learned in these last busy years!"

"Have I?" said Steve, his eyes brightening. "I am especially glad you think I have used my time well, because I can never forget that it was you who taught me my letters,—even how to spell my name," and he turned kindling eyes upon her.

"Did I?" she said, laughing and flushing.

"Yes," he returned, and a bit of tenderness crept into his voice. "I will never forget how you did it, how picturesquely you characterized the various letters for me, how you thought curly S the very prettiest letter in the alphabet, and how disappointed I was when I found my poor name did not hold a single letter which belonged to yours," and there was such deep pathos in the last words, as he looked far into the distance, that she stirred uneasily and could make no answer.

After a moment he went on: "I suppose I read in it, even then, a prophecy of our future, how yours must be separate from mine. There could be nothing in common."

And still she was dumb; not a word came to her lips. But he seemed to need no reply; a sad meditativeness was stealing upon him which made him oblivious for the moment of his surroundings.

But suddenly setting his lips firmly, he turned and said with forced lightness:

"What a bear bachelorhood makes of a man! I have spent so much time alone the last few years that I am already acquiring the bad habit of thinking my thoughts aloud sometimes. Forgive me, won't you?" And he turned to her with more in the tone than the simple words could convey.

"I have nothing to forgive," said she, but with an effort,—which he misinterpreted.

Then gathering her wits she repeated, "I have nothing to forgive, but everything for which to thank you. My starting you in the life intellectual cannot compare with your finding me hanging by a mere thread from a tall tree top and restoring me to the life physical, without which my brilliant intellectual attainments would have been as nothing," she ended gaily, breaking the tension which both had felt.

The talk continued to drift near the sacred realm of the heart, however, until the sanctity of engagement was finally touched upon.

"An engagement is to me a very sacred thing," said Nancy with sweet seriousness, in response to something from Steve. "I have never understood how it could be lightly entered into with only the basis of a brief, gay acquaintance."

Was not that just what she had done? "Oh, consistency, thy name is certainly not woman," thought Steve bitterly. He said:

"Oh, yes, that is good theory, but it is generally overwhelmed by practice when a gay cavalier comes along and takes the maiden heart by storm."

"Perhaps so, with some," returned Nancy quietly, "but so far as I am concerned I do not believe I could be deceived into thinking that a brief, gay acquaintance was sufficient assurance for the binding of two in the tenderest tie of life, when their tastes and ideals might prove to be totally at variance."

Steve's heart leaped within him. Was she trying to tell him something,—to undeceive him with regard to Raymond and herself? Impetuous words rose and trembled on his lips, while the thought raced through his brain that it would not be dishonourable to ask if there were the least hope for him. He would not utter another word if she said the sacred tie was already entered into with Raymond.

But Nancy, in the yielding and yet withdrawing which is characteristic of woman and man never fully understands, plunged into a new topic. Frightened at the plainness of her revelation and almost seeming to divine his purpose, with her brightest talk she led him far afield.

Steve, however, baffled though he was, found memory of that shy look coming back to him insistently, till he suddenly, firmly determined as they rode home once more that Nancy Follet should have the opportunity of accepting or refusing him before he left the place!

XVI

IN THE CRUCIBLE

When Steve and Nancy reached home they found Mr. Follet in bed suffering intensely with sciatic pains. He fretted constantly, declaring he would get up whether or no by afternoon. He was obliged to make a trip into the country for a load of hay, able or not, that evening, he said. Steve offered to go for him, but Mr. Follet impatiently declared that nobody could do it but himself, as there was some other business to be attended to at the same time.

The pain continued so severe, however, that getting up was an impossibility, and about seven o'clock after fretting and fuming for hours, occupying Mrs. Follet and Nancy continually, he said to his wife:

"Go tell Steve to come here."

Mrs. Follet obeyed and brought Steve in from the porch where he sat supposedly reading, Nancy being busy then with the supper dishes.

"Now you go out, ma, and don't come back till I tell you," said Mr. Follet querulously, and his wife went wonderingly.

"Steve," said Mr. Follet as soon as the young man entered, "I know I can trust you, and I am going to get you to do some important business for me."

"I will certainly do anything for you, Mr. Follet, with great pleasure, and I appreciate more than I can tell you the fact that you feel you can trust me," said Steve warmly.

"Well," said Mr. Follet, a little uneasily, "this is mighty partic'ler business I've got. The fact is," he went on with nervous energy, "a part of the world is getting so good it ain't content with just being good itself but is bound and determined that the rest of the world shall do just as it says, and there's a good bit of difference of opinion about what goodness strictly is."

Steve listened a little surprised at the homily. Then Mr. Follet went on:

"I ain't ever cared anything about liquor myself, though I could have had all I wanted all my life long, but I am willing other people should make it, and have it, or sell it, all they want to."

Steve looked more surprised and his lips settled just a little into firmer lines, but Mr. Follet failed to notice it.

"Now, old Kaintuck, which has always been the freest state in the Union, has got a passle o' folks turned loose in it just like the folks I was telling you

- 101 -

about. They're so good themselves they ain't satisfied till they make everybody else do just as they say. They're making laws in the towns that no liquor can be sold, and I tell you men of old Kaintuck ain't goin' to stand that and I don't blame 'em," he concluded vehemently.

Steve started to reply, his lips growing firmer, and his eyes taking fire, but Mr. Follet gave him no chance.

"Now, I promised some fellows that I would meet 'em to-night,—and bring home a load of hay," he ended with an excited laugh.

"A load of hay with whiskey enclosed?" asked Steve, instantly suspecting.

"Yes," said Mr. Follet, delighted with Steve's quickness, "that's the idee. Then I unload it in my barn and ship it as I please to these dry towns. I'm in for the law as a general thing," he added quickly, "but I believe in folks having their rights."

"Well, Mr. Follet," said Steve, going to the foot of the bed and leaning hard upon it, "we must understand each other at once. I do not agree with you as to our rights. I do not think we have the right to destroy ourselves or others with any weapon whatsoever, the pistol, the knife, poison or whiskey. I am with the law in every particular," he said firmly.

"With the law," exclaimed Mr. Follet excitedly, "when it says a man can't do with his own corn on his own place what he wants to do with it? A man's got as good a right, in my mind, to put up a still and make whiskey out of his corn as his wife has to gather apples and make pies!" he concluded, fairly quivering with excitement.

Steve held himself quietly, and said gently:

"Mr. Follet, you are too ill for me to discuss these things with you now. I see we look at them from totally different points of view."

"There ain't but one point of view," shrilly returned Mr. Follet, "and that's the point of view of man's rights. Why, it won't be long till a man can't milk his own cow without the government standing round to watch her switch her tail and tell him how to do it,—all ready to grab the money if he sells a little to a neighbour!"

"Well, Mr. Follet," said Steve, looking steadily but kindly in the enraged eyes of his opponent, "there is one thing that we do agree upon, and that is, every man has a right to his own opinion," and the kindness in Steve's eyes merged into his sudden smile, which stemmed a little the rising tide of Mr. Follet's wrath.

After a somewhat subdued pause he turned to Steve appealingly:

"But you will go and get this load for me,—you will have no responsibility about it. I have never had anything to do with moonshiners before," he went on, "but Raymond got in with 'em and thinks it would be a huge joke to send a lot of their whiskey to his friends in these 'dry towns,' and that prohibition business has riled me so that I promised I would help pass the stuff along. Raymond's going to hang around the saloon and the station to see that the coast is clear o' government men, while the thing is goin' on."

"No," said Steve instantly and firmly when Mr. Follet was through, "I cannot do it, Mr. Follet, greatly as it grieves me to refuse you a favour. I feel that whiskey, the knife and the pistol have been Kentucky's greatest curses, especially among the people of the mountains. I would lay down my life, if necessary, for mountain folks, but I long instead to spend it for them in replacing the pistol and the knife with the book and the pen, and in cultivating among them a thirst for knowledge instead of drink," said Steve with quiet passion which held Mr. Follet's unwilling attention. Then he added:

"Understand me, Mr. Follet, I do not attempt to decide for you what is right or wrong, I only know that I cannot do this thing you ask and keep my self-respect. I must live within the laws of my country even if I should feel sometimes that they are unjust, and I can never take even a remote part in the distribution of whiskey in the land I love," he concluded earnestly.

At this Mr. Follet fairly shouted in a sudden access of rage. He was all the more angry for the moment because in the light of Steve's clear statement he not only felt that Steve was right, but that he himself was wrong.

"Then leave my house this instant with your contemptible idees about Kentucky's rights, and don't dare to stop and speak to my wife or my daughter."

"It is your house, Mr. Follet; I will do just as you say," Steve replied.

Mr. Follet reiterated shrilly:

"Go on out of my house then, and don't you ever come near it again."

Steve bowed and left, not even stopping to get his travelling bag; in fact he forgot he had one, and only caught up his hat from the porch as he passed out.

XVII

FRUITION

Mrs. Follet and Nancy knew that something very exciting was going on between Mr. Follet and Steve and both were exceedingly anxious. When silence took the place of heated discussion they could bear it no longer and went to Mr. Follet's door.

Mrs. Follet had never seen her husband so wrought up before, though he had always been of an exciteable temperament. She did not dare ask a question, but busied herself doing little things for his comfort while Nancy brought in his supper, which he had not wanted earlier and still querulously refused to touch.

A terrible silence settled upon them all. Nancy sat on the porch in distressed wonder over what had happened between her father and Steve, while Mrs. Follet, equally anxious, sat silently by the bed of the restless man. She proposed to get a neighbour to go for the doctor, but Mr. Follet wouldn't hear of it. Hours passed by and then Mr. Follet suddenly started up in bed.

"My God," he cried wildly, "they'll kill him!"

"Who?" cried his wife, starting up also, while Nancy's white face at once appeared in the door.

"Why, Steve," screamed Mr. Follet. "He's gone, and I don't doubt he went straight to old man Greely's for the night. If he did, he's cut across the woods and run into some moonshiners. They'll take him for a government man and shoot him soon's they lay eyes on him!"

He paused for breath, and Mrs. Follet and Nancy were too appalled to speak.

"Do something," screamed Mr. Follet; "I can't have the boy's blood on my hands!"

Then Mrs. Follet with her gentle strength made him quiet down enough to tell them particulars, and she learned that Mr. Follet was to have gone after a load of hay, and coming back would stop at the edge of the wood leading to old man Greely's, walk into the woods a piece to meet the men, and then, if the coast was clear, they'd hide the liquor in the hay load. At the end she said:

"You must go, Nancy——"

"Yes," cried Mr. Follet, "you must go, child, and save Steve. Jim Sutton will know you. They won't touch you, and they'll believe you. I was a fool ever to have anything to do with that moonshine business!"

But Nancy was already out of the room flying for the stable. There was no thought of riding habit or saddle. Throwing a bridle over Gyp's head, she sprang upon his back and like the wind the two rushed forth into the midnight stillness. Would she be in time to save him? It had been so long since he left the house. Oh, would she be too late? She urged Gyp wildly on and on, along the road directly towards the Greely woods, where she would find the moonshiners, and perhaps,—oh, perhaps! God only knew what else she might find.

Every throbbing pulse beat became a prayer that she might be in time to save him.

Meanwhile Steve, upon leaving Mr. Follet, had not gone out into the street, but crossing the lawn into the driveway he went past the stable to the wood back of the house from whence he had come so many years ago. His mind and heart were in a tumult. He scarcely thought where he was going till he suddenly became conscious that he was in the old wood where he had rescued Nancy so long ago. Little Nancy! And he had loved her ever since consciously or unconsciously. But she was completely lost to him now,— that was final. The fair dream-structure which had risen anew that afternoon had fallen again in a tragic moment's space. The mountain blood in Mr. Follet would never forget or forgive. He must leave the place forever. He was adrift again in the world. There would never be tender home ties for him,—he could never love another, no one could be a part of his very self like little Nancy. He dropped down upon a little seat which he had fixed there for her in the old days, and was lost in depressed thought, taking no note of how long he remained.

The stillness of the wood quieted him finally, as it had always done, and he remembered his old friends the Greelys. They would be glad to have him come in for breakfast in the morning, and for the night he would sleep in the Greely woods. He would feel very near to Nancy there, for that spot was hallowed by her memory as no other for him. He rose and made his way over into the road which led to the wood.

It was a brilliant moonlight night, and he walked on under the majestic beauty of the firmament with quieted spirit.

Suddenly, as he had almost reached the wood, he heard rapid hoof-beats behind him and paused to listen, for it was a little-travelled road. Nearer and nearer they came, and then he could distinguish a white dress fluttering in the wind from the flying animal's back and knew the rider must be a woman. The speed of the horse began to slacken as she was almost upon him, and he saw that it was Gyp and Nancy!

She also had recognized him, and the next instant she sprang from the pony and stood beside him.

"Oh, Steve," she panted, "they will kill you!" and stretched her shaking hands out to him. Her agitation was pitiable. Unconsciously he drew her instantly within his arms, while he said with equal unconsciousness:

"Why, Nancy, darling, what do you mean?"

For answer she dropped her head upon his breast and sobbed convulsively.

He held her close, stroking her face and soothing her with tenderest words of love till she was able to speak again.

"The moonshiners that father was to meet, Steve,—they are in the Greely wood, and they will think you are a revenue man and kill you sure," she said brokenly. "You were going there, weren't you?"

"Yes," he said gravely.

"Father thought you would and sent me for you. Oh, it was dreadful, the terror of it," she said shuddering and sobbing anew.

Again he soothed her with caresses and whispered, "But, sweetheart, you know I am not going there now,—not when I can hold you like this." And she nestled in his arms at last in quiet happiness.

Finally she lifted her head and smiled up at him. He turned her face up to the moon's full light and looked longingly into it.

"Nancy, do you love me?" he said.

"Oh, Steve, I've always loved you, I think," she softly replied.

"And it never was Raymond?" he went on insistently, his voice taking on a resonant ring.

"Not in the least," she returned. Then smiling demurely at him she said, "Oh, Steve, you weren't nearly so stupid in learning your letters!"

And he punished her with kisses.

"Do you remember," he said at last tenderly, looking over at the Greely wood, "that you asked me when a little girl to build a house for you and me over there where we might live always?"

"Yes," she said with a touch of sweet reluctance, "I confess I have always remembered that childish speech,—with an intuitive knowledge that I shouldn't have made it, I suppose."

"While I have always treasured it consciously or unconsciously," he returned, with eager joy creeping into the tenderness of his voice. "You were a blessed little prophetess, for it is here under the shadow of the old wood that love has at last built for us the fairest, holiest structure earth ever knew."

Then they remembered the hour of the night and the anxiety of her father and mother, and started back down the road, Nancy saying she would like to walk a little and Steve leading Gyp, who had been unconcernedly grazing by the roadside.

After a time the lover went on again joyously:

"We have equal right to one another now, have we not, sweetheart, for if I saved you from possible death at the moment of our meeting, you have probably saved me from a tragic end to-night. It is the way of our mountain life," he added, his voice taking on a note of sadness; "our joy must always be mingled with tragedy until we learn the beautiful ways of peace."

Then he stopped again and turned her face up to the moonlight once more.

"Will you be content, dearest, to help me in the work I have chosen,—it will probably mean sacrifice,—the giving up of your ambitions."

She smiled back with a low, "More than content, if I may be always with you."

The next day Steve met Raymond on the street, and the latter was more serious than Steve had ever seen him.

"Well, old fellow," he said with an attempt at a smile, "you've licked me again. I know all about the sale of Greely Ridge and your narrow escape last night. Those two things, I admit, show me I am a good deal of a fool, and something of a cad as I used to be. I want you to know that the business with the moonshiners is all off. The other victory you've won over me I can't talk about. I acknowledge you deserve her though, more than I do, and I wish you luck."

Before Steve could reply he went on: "You got some hard knocks when you were a boy, Steve, and they did you good. That is when we need them most.

These are the first real blows I have ever had. I've always been in for a good time and had it, but I don't believe it pays. Father is going to be no end put out with me about the loss of that coal land. I'm going home and make a clean breast of it,—then I am going to clear out. I've decided this morning to write Mr. Polk and see if he has any chance for me there. I know he will give it to me, if he has, for father's sake."

"That is just the thing," said Steve heartily. "I feel sure he can take you in, and the game of business is so interesting there, I know you will like it, and I believe you will make good." He extended his hand with the last words and Raymond took it with a warm clasp.

Mr. Polk's mine was promptly opened up and proved to be a valuable property. In the formation of his company some shares had been placed in the name of Stephen Langly. At the end of two years they began to yield good returns and Steve felt that this, with the income from his work, would make comfort assured for Nancy. Then came a wedding in the Follet home, and just before the company arrived for the ceremony Mr. and Mrs. Polk, her eyes shining as of old, slipped into the little parlour and placed on the carpet, for the bride and groom to stand upon, a beautiful fox-skin rug with a history.

Mr. Follet coming in a moment later nudged his wife excitedly and said:

"Can you tell where under the cano*pee* you ever saw that before?" while she nodded smiling assent.

It caught the eye of Steve as he entered with Nancy on his arm, and he took his place upon it with firm, glad step.

Mr. and Mrs. Polk were obliged to hurry away as soon as the congratulations were over, in order to get back to New York in time for the wedding of Raymond and Nita Trowbridge,—Raymond having well fulfilled Steve's prophecy of making good.

In the fall four years later when the mountains glowed with unusually brilliant colour, as though nature had caught the glory tints of fresh, bright hope for her people, Steve and Nancy opened a new school. Its well-equipped, modern buildings crowned the old wooded mountain of Steve's boyhood, and Steve the second, a sturdy boy, came daily with little Champ to school. The "still" had passed away with the passing of Champ, the elder, in a mountain fight, and a new day had dawned for Hollow Hut.

THE END

CPSIA information can be obtained
at www.ICGtesting.com
Printed in the USA
BVHW070224260122
627120BV00010B/988